P9-EEN-592

What's the difference between a black and a bicycle?
(page 10)

How is transportation being improved in Harlem?
(page 12)

What do you call an Ethiopian with a stubbed toe?
(page 19)

What's the difference between an oyster with epilepsy and a whore with diarrhea?
(page 37)

What's blue and knocks on the window?
(page 90)

How is making love in a canoe like a light beer?
(page 104)

Also by Blanche Knott

Blanche Knott's Truly Tasteless Jokes V

PINNACLE BOOKS   NEW YORK

BLANCHE KNOTT'S TRULY TASTELESS JOKES V

An original Pinnacle Books edition, published for the first time anywhere.

First printing/October 1985

ISBN: 0-523-42487-6
Can. ISBN: 0-523-43457-X

Printed in the United States of America

PINNACLE BOOKS, INC.
1430 Broadway
New York, New York 10018

9 8 7 6 5 4 3 2 1

CONTENTS

Blanche Knott's

TRULY
TASTELESS
JOKES
V

POLISH

Did you hear about the Pole who thought that intercourse was a state highway?

•

How can you tell a Pole from an ape?
  The ape peels the banana before eating it.

•

What do you call a stork who brings Polish babies?
  A dope peddler.

•

Did you hear about the cross-eyed Polish seamstress who couldn't menstruate?

Two Poles decided to try out country living, so they bought a farm complete with all the livestock. The first thing they did was to make sure all the critters were properly housed. They put the dog in the doghouse, the chickens in the coop, the pigs in the pen, and the cows in the barn along with the mule. Everything went smoothly until they reached the door of the mule's stall—the animal's ears kept hitting the top of the doorway, and like any self-respecting mule, he refused to go a step farther.

After talking the problem over, the two Poles decided to jack up the side of the barn and walk the mule into his stall. They had the barn raised up about three inches when a black guy happened by to ask for directions. Seeing what they were doing, he suggested they dig a ditch instead, and walk the mule into his stall.

"Now ain't that typical," said one Pole to the other. "Any fool can see it's the mule's ears that're too long, not his legs."

•

Why did the Pole streak the labor camp?
He heard it was a penal colony.

•

A Pole was working at a construction site where the boss left each day at 11:00 AM and was gone for two hours. This became such a regular occurrence that the rest of the workers decided to spend the two hours in the bar across the street, but the Pole decided to head home for some extra nookie with his wife. When he arrived home, he found his boss busy banging his wife in the bedroom! Well, he walked right out and headed back to the job.

The following day the Pole was working his ass off when everyone headed across to the bar. "Hey, Ski, aren't you coming?" asked one of them.

"Hell, no," said the Pole. "I almost got caught yesterday!"

What does a Pole write on a postcard?

"Hi. Having a great time. Where am I?"

•

This Polish odd-job man was going from door to door in a suburban neighborhood seeing if there was work to be done. An older man answered the doorbell and said that yes, in fact the porch badly need repainting. They agreed on a price, and the Pole was furnished with paint and a brush and shown to the back of the house.

The man was quite pleased when the Pole came around in only two hours and reported the job done. Commenting on the Pole's fast work, he paid him the money and let him out the door. The Pole thanked him and said, "And by the way, that's not a Porsche, that's a Cadillac."

•

Did you hear about the new car insurance in Poland?

It's called "My Fault."

•

How many Poles does it take to start a car?

Five. One to steer, one to work the pedals, two to push, and one to sit under the hood saying, "Va-room, Va-room."

•

How about the Pole who was sent up into space with a monkey? The first day, a red light went on and the monkey took down all the instrument readings. The second day, a red light went on and the monkey took out his slide rule and made all the appropriate calculations. The third day, a green light went on.

"What do I do now?" asked the Pole.

"Feed the monkey," said a little voice from Earth.

What do you call twenty-five Polish women in a swimming pool?
    Bay of Pigs.

•

What's a goof ball?
    A Polish formal dance.

•

Did you hear about the Polish football team?
    They were on the other team's two-yard line, and the quarterback faded back sixty yards to throw the bomb.

•

A Polish couple and a single man are shipwrecked on a desert island. It doesn't take long for the single guy to get pretty horny, and finally he comes up with an idea for getting into the wife's pants. Climbing way up a tall palm tree, he hollers back down to the couple, "Hey y'all, quit fucking down there!" The Pole looks over at his wife—who's standing ten feet away—and says, "What the hell's he talking about?"
    This goes on for several hours, until the married man is overcome with curiosity and decides to climb up the palm to see for himself what the other guy's problem is. As he's going up, the horny fellow jumps down to the beach, grabs the wife, and proceeds to screw her like crazy.
    The Pole finally reaches the top where the single guy had been, looks down, and says, "Goddamn if he wasn't right—it does look like they're fucking down there!"

•

Did you hear they had to ban "the wave" from Tiger Stadium?
    Too many Poles were drowning.

How about the Polish wetsuit?
  It's made of chain link.

•

How about the Polish girl whose boyfriend said he loved her?
  She believed him.

•

Did you hear the two biggest Polish lies?
  1) The check is in my mouth.
  2) I won't come in your mail.

•

How can you tell the Polish secretary?
  She's the one with Wite-Out all over her computer screen.

•

How do you stop a Polish amphibious landing?
  Shoot their rubber horses.

•

A Pole walks into a travel agency and demands the special
Hawaiian tour. The travel agent says fine, but first, the Pole
must fill out some forms in the office next door. Just as the
Pole gets through the door, someone hits him over the head,
throws him in the corner, and mugs him.
  Later that day, an Italian walks into the same travel agency
and asks for the same special Hawaiian tour. Again, the travel
agent explains about the forms and sends him to the office
next door. As soon as the Italian opens the door, he gets hit
on the head, thrown in the corner, and mugged.
  When the two of them wake up, they find themselves floating in the middle of the ocean on a small raft. The Italian looks
over at the Pole and says, "I wonder if they'll fly us back?"
  The Pole responds knowingly, "They didn't last year."

What does a Polish bridegroom say on his wedding night?
"Where's the Reset button?"

•

How do you tell a Polish ladder from a normal one?
The Polish one has the word STOP stenciled on the top rung.

•

A Pole is walking down the street and passes a hardware store advertising a sale on a chainsaw that is capable of cutting 700 trees in seven hours. The Pole thinks that's a great deal and decides to buy one.

The next day, he comes back with the saw and complains to the salesman that the thing didn't come close to chopping down the 700 trees the ad said it would.

"Well," said the salesman, "let's test it out back."

Finding a log, the salesman pulls the starter cord and the saw makes a great roaring sound.

"What's that noise?" asks the Pole.

•

What's the National Tree of Poland?
The telephone pole.

BLACK

What do you call a black midget in Ireland?
  A lepra-coon.

•

One Saturday three little black kids were sitting around wondering what the meanest animal in the world is. LeMoyne says it's a tiger; Tyrone insists it's a lion. "You bof wrong," maintains Leroy. "It's a crocogator."

"You mean an alligator?"

"Nossir."

"Then what he look like?" ask the other two.

"At one end he got de haid of a crocodile," explains Leroy, "and at the other, de haid of an alligator."

"Den how he shit?" demands LeMoyne triumphantly.

"He don' shit—dat's what make him so mean!"

7

This man was sitting on a park bench with his pet raccoon on his shoulder when a black guy walked up to him. "What kinda animal is that?" he asked.

"That's what you've been called all your life" was the reply.

"Oh," said the black, "so *that's* a motherfucker."

•

What do you get when you cross a black and a Jew?
A janitor in a law firm.

•

Who was the first black prostitute?
Kunta Kinte's sister—Rentacunta.

•

Did you hear General Motors has issued a recall of its 1982 Eldorado?
A watermelon won't fit in the glove compartment.

•

The third-grade teacher was giving a lesson on farms. "What's this, class?" she asked, holding up a picture, and the class chorused, "It's a rake."

"Very good. And what's this?"

"A tractor," replied the class.

"Good. And this?" Silence from the third grade. "Well, children," said the teacher, "pay attention. This is a hoe."

"Ain't no hoe, teacher," spoke up little Titus. "My sister's a hoe, and she don' look nuthin' like that."

•

Did you hear that the local police are doing away with their German Shepherd dogs?

Since they haven't had any trouble with the Germans in forty years, they're going to replace them with coonhounds.

How about the Japanese factory that spray-painted all their new robots black?

They were two hours late to work the next day.

•

What do you call ten blacks butt-fucking?

Soul Train.

•

A little black brother and sister were out trick-or-treating and came to the door of an imposing Colonial house. "And who are you?" boomed the big white man who came to the door.

"We're Jack and Jill," said the brother.

"You can't be Jack and Jill—you're black," said the man, and shut the door.

The boy and girl came back a few minutes later, dressed differently. "Who are you this time?" asked the man.

"Hansel and Gretel," piped up the little girl.

"You can't be Hansel and Gretel—you're black," boomed the man.

The brother and sister rang the doorbell a third time, naked this time around. "Who are you *now*?" he asked.

"We're M & M's," she explained. "I'm plain, and he's with nuts."

•

Why don't blacks like enemas?

They turn transparent.

•

What does a Valley Girl say after going down on a black man?

"Gag me with a coon!"

Once there was a hooker who had quite a reputation—she said she could melt any man's balls, just with her hands. A couple of guys go over to her place to check it out. She plays with the first guy's balls for a couple of minutes and, sure enough, they start to melt. It doesn't even take that long to have the same effect on the second guy. Then up steps a big black man and pulls out his nuts.

The hooker rubs them and strokes them and tickles them but absolutely nothing happens. "Say," she asks, "how come this worked on those other fellas but not on you?"

He smiles and says, " 'Cause chocolate melts in your mouth, not on your hands."

•

What's the definition of "indiscreet"?
Where a black parks his car.

•

What's the difference between a black and a bicycle?
A bicycle doesn't sing, "Kumbaya, my Lord" when you chain it to the wall.

•

What goes black-pink-black-pink-black-pink?
A black jerking off.

•

What are six words you never ever want to hear?
"Hi, I be yo' new neighbor."

•

Leroy and Jasper have just been promoted from privates to sergeants. Not long after, they're out for a walk and Leroy says, "Hey, Jasper, there's the Officer's Club. Let's you and me stop in."

"But we's privates," protests Jasper.

"We's sergeants now," says Leroy, pulling him inside. "Now, Jasper, I'se gonna sit down and have me a drink."

"But we's privates," says Jasper.

"You blind?" asks Leroy, pointing at his stripes. "We's sergeants now." So they have their drink, and pretty soon a hooker comes up to Leroy. "You're cute," she says, "and I'd like to screw you, but I've got a bad case of gonorrhea."

Leroy pulls his friend to the side and whispers, "Jasper, go look in the dictionary and see what that 'gonorrhea' means. If it's okay, give me the okay sign." So Jasper goes to look it up, comes back, and gives Leroy the big okay sign.

Three weeks later Leroy is laid up in the infirmary with a terrible case of gonorrhea. "Jasper," he says, "what fo' you give me an okay?"

"Well, Leroy, in the dictionary, it say gonorrhea affects only the privates." He points to his stripes. "But we's sergeants now."

•

What was the first government-subsidized housing project?
    Uncle Tom's Cabin.

•

What do you get when you cross a black and a fish?
    Filet of soul brother.

•

At 7:00 PM a big bruiser would walk into the local bar and shout, "I can whip anybody in the house!" This was true but tiresome, and the bartender's hopes picked up when one day at 6:45 a man walked in with a gorilla that was smoking a cigar. "First time I ever saw a gorilla smoking a cigar," commented the bartender. "Say, is he dangerous?"

"When he's with me, he's a kitten," says the owner, "but if I left him alone, he'd tear you to pieces."

The bartender proceeds to strike a deal with the gorilla's

owner—a couple of drinks for him and a couple of cigars for the gorilla if he'll just leave the gorilla in the men's room with the lights out for a little while. So that's where the gorilla is when the bully comes in at 7:00 and shouts, "I can whip anybody in the house!"

"Not tonight you can't," says the bartender cheerfully. "Check out the fellow in the men's room."

The bruiser heads right for the bathroom and a hell of a racket follows. A little later he emerges, only slightly the worse for wear, saying, "Goddammit—give a nigger a fur coat and a cigar and he thinks he can whip anybody!"

•

What do you call a baby nigger?
    A nigglet.

•

What's black and white and sees eye-to-eye with Moshe Dayan?
    Sammy Davis, Jr.

•

How is transportation being improved in Harlem?
    They're planting the trees closer together.

•

A man walked into the Post Office and reported that a mail truck had been stolen. Thanking him for his concern, the Postmaster asked how he knew that the truck had been ripped off.

"It musta been," said the man, "because there was a white man driving it."

•

After a prayer meeting on a fine spring evening, a black preacher was walking home one of the sisters in his congregation. "You know, sister," he commented, "you're the third sister I've walked home that's pregnant."

"Why, I'm not pregnant," she exclaimed.

The preacher replied, "You ain't home yet, either."

•

Two little black girls were walking down the street when one asked the other, "How old is you?"

"I don't know" was the answer.

"Well, what's your favorite thing in the whole world?"

"Sweet 'tater" was the prompt response.

"You's ten."

•

Three blacks went into business for themselves. Said the first, "I put up 65% of the capital, so I'm the president and chairman of the board."

"I put up 30% of the money," said the second, "so I'm appointing myself vice president, secretary, and treasurer.

"Well, I put up 5%," pointed out the third partner. "What's that make me?"

The chairman said, "I'm appointing you vice president of sex and music."

"That sounds mighty fine," said the third man, "but what's it mean?"

"It means that when I want your fucking advice, I'll whistle."

•

A black girl came home from fifth grade and told her mother she had a case of the clap. Her mother said, "Put it in the refrigerator, honey, your Daddy'll drink anything."

•

After the War, a Yankee general bought himself a plantation down South which he really loved. Every Saturday night he'd throw a big party for his Southern friends, but somebody would always yell out "Damn Yankee" at some point, and this really upset the general. Finally, a friend confided in him that people would stop calling him a damn Yankee if he'd make love to a black girl.

So the very next day he went down to the colored part of town, found himself an attractive black girl, and they went to bed. In the heat of their lovemaking, she screamed, "Ooh, you damn Yankee!"

The furious general stopped midstroke and demanded to know how she knew he was a Yankee.

Smiling winsomely, she said, " 'Cause dem Southern boys don't kiss me like you do."

•

Why do kids like white teachers better than black ones?
Because it's easier to carry an apple to school than a watermelon.

•

Did you hear about the ten-year-old black girl who was afraid of flies—until she opened one?

•

Why was the wheelbarrow invented?
So blacks would learn to walk on their hind legs.

•

A black woman walked into a bank to make a substantial deposit. The clerk inquired, "Did you hoard all this money yourself?"

"No," she said, "my sister whored half of it."

Under pressure from civil rights activists, NASA agreed to start recruiting black astronauts. At first their motto was, "A Coon on the Moon by June," but things fell behind schedule and they had to change it to "The Jig Is Up."

•

Why do black woman make such good housekeepers?
   Built-in Brillo pads.

•

What is it called when you get mugged by 600 blacks?
   High blood pressure.

•

How do you make a perfect Manhattan?
   Move Union Carbide to Harlem.

•

What are the colors on the Afro-American flag?
   Red for pulp, black for seeds, and green for the rind of a watermelon.

JEWISH

Did you hear about the sequel to *Jaws* about a loan shark?
  It's called *Jews*.

•

A young Jewish man takes his mother to a movie about life in ancient Rome. She's from the old country and has a little difficulty following the customs in this strange land, so at one point she asks her son to explain a scene in progress. "This particular scene," he whispers, "shows how in those days the Romans often persecuted the Christians by throwing them in the arena to be devoured by lions."
  Studying the gory image for a few moments, she points her finger at a lion in the far corner and shouts, "And dat vun—vy isn't he eating?"

•

How do you know if a JAP is a nymphomaniac?
  She has to have a man at least once a month.

Her daughter the anthropologist has been off in darkest Africa for fourteen months and has just announced her engagement to the man of her dreams. So the Jewish mother is almost beside herself with excitement when they arrive at the airport in time for the holidays. Seeing her daughter come through the gate accompanied by a huge black man with a bone through his nose, clad only in a grass skirt and bead necklace, for a moment she is struck speechless. Then she sobs, "Oh, Rachel, I wanted for you a rich doctor, not a witch doctor!"

•

What's a Jewish porno film?
  Ten minutes of sex, fifty minutes of guilt.

•

How about the new disease affecting Jewish women?
  It's called MAIDS—if they don't get one, they die.

•

Why did the Jew cross the road?
  To franchise the other side.

•

What's the Jews' favorite parade?
  The March of Dimes.

•

How do you give a JAP an orgasm?
  Scream, "Charge it to Daddy!"

•

Why do JAPs use Tampax instead of sanitary napkins?
  Because nothing goes in without a string attached.

Did you hear about the JAP who asked her father for fifty dollars to go shopping?

"Forty dollars," he screamed, "what're you gonna buy with thirty dollars?"

ETHIOPIAN

Who's the patron saint of Ethiopia?
   Karen Carpenter.

·

What's the fastest animal in the world?
   The Ethiopian chicken.

·

What food do you never see in Ethiopia?
   After-dinner mints.

·

What do you call an Ethiopian wearing a turban?
   A Q-Tip.
With a stubbed toe?
   A three-iron.
With buck teeth?
   A rake.

19

Why do Ethiopians give such good head?
  They'll swallow anything.

●

What's this? [Hold up a blank piece of paper.]
  An Ethiopian menu.

●

What do you call an Ethiopian with sesame seeds on his head?
  A quarter-pounder.

●

What's black and has cobwebs?
  An Ethiopian's asshole.

●

Did you hear about the big sale of Venetian blinds to Ethiopia?
  They're using them for bunk beds.

●

If two dogs are a herd, what do you call an Ethiopian with five dogs?
  A caterer.

●

What do Yoko Ono and the Ethiopians have in common?
  Living off dead beetles.

What do you call an Ethiopian with a dime on his head?
  A nail.

•

What do children in Ethiopia get for their birthday?
  Flies.
For Christmas?
  Buried.

•

What do you call a seventy-five-pound Ethiopian?
  "Fatso."

•

What was the score of the American-Ethiopian soccer game?
  America 8, Ethiopia didn't.

•

Definition of an optimist:
  An Ethiopian in a dinner jacket.

•

How many Ethiopians can you fit in a shower?
  It's hard to tell—they keep slipping down the drain.

•

How many Ethiopians can you fit in a phone booth?
  All of them.

Why did the Ethiopian have a mouthful of dirt?
He was training to be a javelin.

•

What's 6–13–6?
The measurements of Miss Ethiopia.

WASP

What's a WASP's idea of post-coital depression?
  Sitting on a floating chair in his private pool and not being able to reach his martini.

•

What do you call a female WASP with a pedigree who loves to suck cock?
  DARling.

•

When a WASP wants to suck your cock, what do you do?
  Wash it.

•

What did the WASP say to the black?
  "Come here."
What did the black man say back?
  "But it tastes *so* good."

What did the WASP say to the Pole?
  "Come here."
What did the Pole say back?
  "I thought I already did."

What did the WASP say to the Puerto Rican?
  "Come here."
What did the Puerto Rican say back?
  "Turn over, mamasita."

·

A bee is checking out a clover patch when he comes across another bee who's wearing a yarmulke. "Why in hell are you wearing that Jewish skullcap?" he asks.
  Says the first bee, "Well, I don't want to be taken for a WASP."

·

How many WASPs does it take to change a light bulb?
  Six. One to change the bulb and five to write the environmental impact report.

·

Two WASPy ladies were out for a walk trying to outsnob each other. "In Boston," says one, "we place our emphasis entirely on breeding."
  "In Philadelphia, we think it's a lot of fun, but we do other things too," says the other.

·

What do you get when you cross a black and a WASP?
  An abortion.

Why don't they use WASPs to pick cotton?
  They might get lost.

•

What does a WASP get when her car won't start?
  A very emotionally upsetting day.

ETHNIC VARIEGATED

What do you call a picnic in Madrid?
A spicnic.

·

A Pole was so proud of his new red Cadillac that he just had to show it off, so he cruised through the black part of town. At a stop light, a giant black hauled him out of the driver's seat, drew a circle around him in the road, and told him not to step out of the circle unless he wanted to get the shit beat out of him.

The black guy started to demolish the Caddie, starting with the headlights and windows when he heard the Pole laughing. He moved on to the body and engine, but in between crashes he couldn't help hearing the Pole's hysterical giggles. Finally the black guy came over with his crowbar and said, "What in hell you laughin' at? Your fancy car's never gonna run again."

Snickering, the Pole replied, "So? Ever since you've been tearing up my car, I've been stepping in and out of this circle."

What do you get when you cross a Mexican with a faggot?
  A señor-eater.

•

What do you call 2000 pounds of Oriental soup?
  Won ton.

•

I have good news and bad news:
  The bad news is that the Martians have landed in California, and they eat blacks and piss gas;
  The good news is that they're headed East.

•

Hear about the Great Wall of China?
  It has chinks in it.

•

This is the story of the Italian who went to Detroit:
  One day I'ma go to a bigga hotel in Detroit. I goa down toa breakfast and say to da waitress, "I want two piss of toast." She only branga me one piss, so I say, "Heya, waitress, I wanta two piss." She say to go to the restroom. I say, "You no understand, I wanta two piss on da plate." She say, "You better not piss on the plate, you sonna ma bitch!" And I don't even know her!
  Later I goa toa lunch atta restaurant. The waitress branga me a spoon anna knife but no fock, so I say, "Heya, waitress, I wanna fock." She say everybody wanna fock. I say, "You no understand, I wanna fock on the table." She say, "You better not fock on the table, you sonna ma bitch!" And I don't even know da lady!
  Later I goa toa my room, but there'sa only one sheet on da bed. I tell da manager, "I want two sheet," and he tella me to go to da toilet. When I explain, he say, "You better not shit on the bed, you sonna ma bitch!"

Finally I goa toa check out. I'ma leavin' and da man at da desk say, "Peace to you." I say, "Piss on you, too, you sonna ma bitch! I go back to Italy!"

•

The inspector is conducting his annual inspection of an under-wear factory when he notices that the shipments are being packaged in lots of fives, sevens, and twelves. Curious, he asks the factory manager why this is so.

"It's all marketing," explains the manager. "The fives are for the Germans, who change their underwear five days out of seven. The sevens are for the Americans and Canadians, who change their underwear every day of the week. The twelves, they're for the Italians."

"And why is that?" asks the inspector.

"Well, you got January, February . . ."

•

What does a WASP do when his car breaks down?
    Calls the nearest Chevrolet dealership.
What does a black do when his car breaks down?
    Calls the nearest Cadillac dealership.
And what does a Jew do when his car breaks down?
    Puts a FOR SALE sign in the window and takes a cab to the nearest Hilton.

•

What's an Italian mother's very greatest fear for her daughter?
    Anorexia nervosa.

•

The wealthy Iranian tourist was outraged at being searched by Customs on his arrival at JFK Airport. "New York is the asshole of the world!" he screamed.

"Yessir," said the customs official. "Are you just passing through?"

A Frenchman, an American, and a Pole are going on a drive through the countryside when their car breaks down. A few miles down the road they come across a farm and are offered shelter for the night. Showing them to a room, the farmer says, "Just don't stick your dicks in those three holes."

But horniness and curiosity overwhelm the visitors in the middle of the night; the Frenchman sticks his dick in the first hole, the Amerian in the second, and the Pole in the third.

"Okay, wise guys, who used the holes?" asked the farmer the next morning.

"The first one was *magnifique*," exlaims the Frenchman. "What was eet?"

"My wife's pussy," said the farmer.

The American confessed to the second, saying how nice and tight it has been. "That's good," said the farmer. "That was my daughter's pussy."

The Pole, whose dick was all bandaged up, said, "The third hole was great, but after a while it began to hurt like hell. What was it?"

The farmer says, "A milking machine that doesn't stop till it gets five quarts."

•

How do you confuse an Irish road worker?
   Give him two shovels and tell him to take his pick.

•

Fabio and Nunzio rent a private plane for the day and are doing fine until it's time for touchdown. Fabio is busy with all the instrument readings and finally gets the plane down, but has to screech to a stop. "Boy, that's a short runway," he says, wiping his forehead.

"Yes," agrees Nunzio, "but look how wide it is."

•

What do you get when you cross a Mexican and a Spaniard?
   Spic and Span.

A young Indian decides to celebrate his eighteenth birthday by losing his virginity, so he walks into town to the local whorehouse. "Me want screw," he explains to the madam, who asks him if he's had any experience. Pointing him to a tree in the yard, she tells him to get some practice on a convenient knothole first.

A week later, the brave again presents himself and his desire to the madam, who recognizes him and shows him up to one of the whores' rooms. "And what would you like?" asks the prostitute coyly. "Takem off all clothes," he says. She smiles and undresses, then obeys his next instruction to bend over. Eyeing her suspiciously, he takes a big piece of wood and smacks her across the ass. Jumping up, she screams, "What the hell was that for?"

The Indian looks at her and says, "Me check for bees."

•

What do you call a gay Hispanic?
   A Spiggot.

•

What do you call a taco shell with a food stamp inside it?
   A Mexican fortune cookie.

•

Why aren't there any Puerto Rican astronauts?
   Because they'd honk the horn, squeal the tires, and play the radio too loud all the way to the moon.

•

This Midwesterner was enjoying his vacation in Sicily when he came across a roadblock manned by an armed bandit. Ordering him out of his rent-a-car, the bandit commanded him to masturbate. I can think of worse fates, thought the tourist as he dutifully obeyed. The bandit told him to do it again and the tourist complied, though it took a bit longer.

"Again," commanded the Sicilian, ignoring his victim's protests and waving his gun around, and the fellow finally managed to jerk off a third time.

"Okay," said the bandit. "Now-a my sister ride with you to town."

•

What do Italian mothers do when their children misbehave?
    They wop them.

•

And what kind of hamburgers do Italians eat?
    Woppers!

•

How do Chinese mothers name their babies?
    Throw some silverware down the stairs and name them after the noise it makes.

•

A young boy was born to a Jewish woman and a black man, and one day he came home from school with a serious question: was he more Jewish or more black? His mother said she didn't know and to ask his daddy when he came home from work. The little boy's daddy insisted on knowing why he needed to know.

The little boy explained that the kid down the street had a bike for sale. He wanted to know if he should try to bargain him down on the price, or just wait till after dark and steal it.

•

What do you call Japanese cunnilingus?
    Constluctive clitisism.

What are Mexicans?
   Living proof that Indians fucked buffaloes.

•

Why is there such a dearth of great Mexican literature?
   Spray paint wasn't invented till 1949.

•

What do you get when you cross the *Texas Chainsaw Massacre* with a group of Eskimos?
   Cold cuts.

•

How does the U.S. Board of Immigration classify Mexicans who are living legally in the U.S.?
   Canadians.

•

Did you hear about the new Italian steel belted radial tires?
   Dago forward, dago backward and when dago flat, dago wop, wop, wop, wop.

•

Two Poles couldn't figure out how to measure a flagpole they'd been hired to paint by the foot, so they asked a black man who was passing by if he would help.
   The black pulled a pin from the bottom of the pole, laid the pole on the ground, pulled out his ruler, and measured it. When he was finished, he put his tape measure away, put the flag pole back in its stand, and left.
   Once out of earshot, the one Polack turned to the other and said, "Isn't it just like a nigger, you ask for the height and he gives you the width."

Why aren't there any Mexican astronauts?

Because whenever they hear the word "launch," they go out to eat.

•

An American, a Pole, and a Chinaman were working in the coal mines. The American was in charge of digging, the Pole was in charge of shoveling, and the Chinaman was responsible for supplies.

The American discovered he needed some more tools, so he sent the Chinaman to go get them. Two hours later, the Chinaman hadn't returned so the other two went looking for him. As they rounded a corner in the mine shaft, the Chinaman jumped out from behind a pillar and yelled, *"Supplies!"*

•

Who killed more Indians than Custer?

Union Carbide.

•

Have you heard the new Union Carbide corporate song?

"One little, two little, three little Indians . . ."

•

A Texan and a Pole were transporting several prize cows aboard a twin-engine plane. When one of the engines sputtered and died, and the plane began to tilt, the Pole commented, "If that other engine goes, we're gonna crash."

Sure enough, a minute later the second engine gave out. In a panic the Pole shouted, "What're we gonna do? We're going down."

"Don't worry," said the Texan calmly.

"Don't worry! What about your family?"

"Don't have any," said the Texan.

"What about the cows?"

"Fuck the cows!"

"Gee," said the Pole, "have we got time for that?"

•

Two traveling salesmen, a Frenchman and an Irishman, asked for a room overnight at a lonely farmhouse after their car had broken down. The elderly farmer agreed to take them in, saying, "I'll let you stay as long as you don't go near my daughter's bed." And he sprinkled the floor around her bed with popcorn so he'd be able to hear if anyone went near.

In the middle of the night the Frenchman was no longer able to bear the thought of the farmer's beautiful daughter lying alone. Tiptoeing to her door, he peed all over the popcorn so it wouldn't make any noise and proceeded to have a delightful time with the young woman.

The next morning the two salesmen were comparing notes. "Man, that girl was the best lay I've had in a long, long time," said the Frenchman.

"No doubt about that," said the Irishman, "and the buttered popcorn wasn't bad either."

HANDICAPPED

What's the definition of agony?
A one-armed man hanging off the edge of a cliff with an attack of jock itch.

•

Why did the leper go to the political rally?
Because he wanted to give somebody a piece of his mind.

•

What did Helen Keller say as she was making love to her new boyfriend?
"Funny, you don't feel Jewish."

•

What's Helen Keller's favorite song?
"The Sound of Sound."

Doctor (taking up his stethoscope): "Big breaths."
   Patient: "Yeth, and I'm not even thixteen."

•

What do you call a midget fortune-teller who escapes from prison?
   A small medium at large.

•

Driving cross-country, this fellow ran out of gas in the middle of nowhere. He could hardly believe his luck when, after only a few miles, the telephone wires led him to a little house. When no one answered after ten minutes of banging on the door, he turned to leave, only to see something curious through the living room window. There stood a nude couple facing each other, the women squeezing her tits and the man beating his dick with an umbrella.

After watching for a while, the guy wrote them off as loonies and went next door to try his luck. The neighbors were friendly, and after he'd called for a tow truck, the guy couldn't resist describing what he'd seen in the first house.

The woman laughed and said, "Oh, they carry on that conversation all the time."

"What do you mean?" asked the puzzled traveler.

"Well, you see, they're a deaf couple. She was asking her husband to milk the cow and he was saying, 'Fuck you, bitch, it's raining!' "

•

Did you hear Barney Clark's favorite new song?
   It's called "How Can You Mend a Broken Heart?"

•

What's the disadvantage of visiting a leper prostitute?
   She can only give head once.

What's the advantage of being visited by a leper prostitute?
    She leaves so much behind for you to remember her by.

•

Where can a midget spend the night without paying?
    A Stayfree Minipad.

•

How did Helen Keller die?
    She tried to read a player piano.

•

What did the impotent man and the frigid woman accomplish
in bed together?
    A bilateral freeze.

•

What's the difference between an oyster with epilepsy and a
whore with diarrhea?
    One you shuck between fits . . .

•

I'll say one thing about polio—
    It keeps the kids off the streets.

•

What's very small and crawls into walls?
    Helen Keller's baby.

•

How do you make a Venetian blind?
    Poke him in the eye.

How did Helen Keller's teacher keep her from talking in class?
　　Made her wear mittens.

•

Did you hear about the new jokes for the deaf?
　　[Remain silent.]

•

What does a woman say to a blind man in bed?
　　"Cum here, cum here!"

•

How did Helen Keller cut off her hand?
　　Reading the stop sign at 55 mph.

•

What did one leper say to the other?
　　"Haven't seen much of you around here lately."

•

How do you circumcise a leper?
　　Shake him.

•

Remember what you say to a one-legged hitchhiker?
　　"Hop in!"
So what do you say to a no-legged hitchhiker?
　　"Need a lift?"

What do you call a dog with three legs?
  Tippy.

                        •

What do you call a guy with no arms and no legs hanging
from a tree?
  Barry.

In a grave?
  Doug.

Wrapped around a telephone pole?
  Curly.

With three eyes?
  Seymour.

If a guy with no arms and no legs in a pile of leaves is
called Russell, what do you call this same person two weeks
later?
  Pete.

If you call a guy with no arms and no legs Dick, what do you
call his preppy armless and legless girlfriend?
  Muffy.

What do you call a girl with no arms and no legs trying to
climb the stairs?
  Patience.

At the beach?
  Sandy.

                        •

Did you hear about the fellow with two wooden legs?
  He caught fire and burnt to the ground.

What is a leper's favorite rock and roll song?
  "Footloose."

•

How did Helen Keller's parents punish her?
  They covered the toilet bowl with Saran Wrap.

CELEBRITIES

How did Dolly Parton get two black eyes?
  She went jogging and forgot to wear a bra.

•

Why is Michael Jackson's voice so high?
  He moonwalks with his legs crossed.

•

Why wasn't JFK a good boxer?
  He couldn't take a shot to the head.

•

Know why the National Hockey League drafted Indira Gandhi?
  She stopped seven shots in four seconds.

What do Alex Haley and Suzanne Somers have in common?
  Black roots.

•

A lonely woman eagerly waited for Santa to show up on
Christmas Eve. When he finally scrambled out of the chimney
into her living room, she asked, "Santa, will you please stay
with me?"
  "Ho, ho, ho," said Santa, "got my presents to deliver."
  The woman took off her robe and repeated her request.
  "Ho, ho, ho," said Santa, "gotta go, gotta go."
  The woman took off her negligee, slipped out of her pant-
ies, began to stroke her pussy, and whispered, "Santa, won't
you please stay with me?"
  Santa replied, "Ho, ho, ho, gotta stay—can't get up the
chimney with my dick this way!"

•

Know why Mondale nominated Geraldine Ferraro as his running mate?
  He didn't want Reagan to be the only one with a bush on
his ticket.

•

What did Jesse Jackson say when he was asked about Beirut?
  "Pretty good, but Hank Aaron was better."

•

What was John Lennon's last hit?
  The pavement.

•

Did you hear who was nominated Weight Watchers' "Man of
the Year"?
  Bobby Sands.

What do you get when you cross Richard Pryor and Ella Fitzgerald?

Cinderella.

•

Did you see the new movie out starring O.J. Simpson and Barbra Streisand?

It's called *Rentl*.

•

Did you hear Dennis Wilson and Natalie Wood are forming their own musical group?

The Beached Boys.

•

What do you call E.T. with no morals?

E.Z.

•

President Reagan was returning in Air Force One from a trip to Central America when the pilot advised him that they were putting down at Homestead AFB for about twenty minutes to refuel. Deciding to take the opportunity to stretch his legs and take a leak, Reagan walked over to the latrine and found himself at a urinal next to a very large black sergeant. Unable to resist comment, the President asked, "Say, Sergeant, how in the hell do you get one that big?"

"It's easy enough, suh," said the sergeant. "You puts it in easy, you takes it out easy, and you jus' keeps it up—that's all there is to it."

The President could hardly wait till all the welcoming ceremonies were over with at the White House before trying out his newfound rhythm on Nancy. But after a couple of easy ins and easy outs, Nancy sat up and exclaimed, "Ronnie, for God's sake—will you quit fucking like a nigger!"

If Castro were gay, what would you call his lover?
  An infidel.

•

What would you get if you crossed a gorilla with a computer?
  A Hairy Reasoner.

•

Why is Prince Charles's dick blue?
  Because he dipped it in Royal Di.

•

What do you get when you cross Billie Jean King with Bo Derek?
  A DC-10.

•

What's this [a twisted-up paperclip]?
  The Bionic Woman's pubic hair.

•

What do Richard Pryor, Michael Jackson, and Hot Lips Hoolihan have in common?
  Major burns.

•

What's the name of Michael Jackson's new album?
  Griller.

•

How are McDonald's and the White House alike?
  They're both run by clowns named Ronald.

What's grosser than gross?
Watching Nancy and Ronald Reagan screwing.

•

What kind of birth control does Spock use?
A vulcanized rubber.

•

How did the ewok get from Atlanta to Los Angeles in just three days?
Squashed on the windshield of a Greyhound bus.

•

How did Princess Leia get a sore butt?
She sat on Darth Vader's face.

•

What's the difference between Darth Vader's prick and his laser sword?
His prick gets hard and hot when *he* gets turned on.

•

What do the Ayatollah Khomeini's buddies think of him?
They all think he's a hot Shiite.

•

Did you hear they're building an archive for the Nixon papers?
No admission charge—but you have to break in.

•

What would Grace Kelly be doing if she were alive today?
The backstroke.

They say Prince Rainier didn't lose his style . . .
Just his Grace.

•

Why doesn't Santa Claus's wife have any children?
Because Santa only comes once a year, and he always has a bag.

•

Did you hear that Willie Nelson got run over by a Mack truck?
Yeah, he's singing "On the Road Again."

•

Why did Vanessa Williams lose her job as Miss America?
They didn't like her eating habits.

•

Why did Karen Carpenter shoot her dog?
It kept trying to bury her.

CRUELTY TO ANIMALS

Why do male dogs smell female dogs' asses?
  Female dogs have no pussies to lick.

•

A little boy came in the house and said, "Mommy, how much air does an Airedale need?"
  "I don't know," she answered. "Why?"
  "Because I just saw one pumping up another one."

•

What goes "Hoppity . . . clank . . . hoppity . . . clank?"
  The Easter Bunny with polio.

•

Once there was this city boy who wanted to go country, so he headed out to a farm to buy some animals. "I'll take one of these," he said to the farmer. "What is it?"

"Well, to me it's a cock, but to you it's a rooster," said the farmer.

"I'll take one of these, too," said the city boy. "What is it?"

"Well, to me it's a pullet, but to you it's a chicken," replied the farmer.

"Okay," said the city boy. "And I'll take one of those, too, if you'll tell me what it is."

"To me it's an ass, but to you it's a mule," explained the farmer, "and when that ass gets stubborn, it sits down and you have to scratch its belly to get it moving again."

So the city boy set off down the road with all his new purchases. He was doing fine till a pretty girl drove by, at which point the ass sat down and refused to budge. Seeing he was having some trouble, the girl backed up and asked if there was anything she could do to help.

"Actually, yes," said the city boy. "Will you hold my cock and pullet while I scratch my ass?"

•

Did you hear about the female tuna fish?
  She smelled like a woman from Poland.

•

What did the grape do when the elephant sat on it?
  It let out a little wine.

•

Why do mice have such small balls?
  They can't dance.

•

A fourteen-year-old Californian was visiting his Cajun relatives in Louisiana for the summer. His coon-ass cousin of about the same age was showing him around the bayous when they came across a sheep stuck in a barbed-wire fence.

"Boy, I wish that was Linda Evans," said the Californian kid.

The lil' coon-ass looked around and said, "I just wish it was dark."

•

Arab saying: A woman for sons, a boy for pleasure, and a goat for sheer ecstasy.

•

Australia: Where men are men and sheep are nervous.

•

What's grosser than gross?

One dog giving a blow job to another dog.

•

The old rooster could never get enough. He screwed every chicken in the barnyard and wore them all out, so the farmer put him in with the ducks. Pretty soon all the ducks were begging for a rest, so the farmer tethered the rooster out in a cornfield. After a while the farmer looked out his window and saw that the bird was lying on the ground and looked dead as a doornail. Going out to check, he found the rooster lying down all right, but with its eyes wide open. "What's the matter?" he asked.

"*Shhhhh*," hissed the rooster, motioning upward with the tip of a wing. "Turkey vultures!"

•

What do you call a rabbit with herpes?

Peter Rotten Tail.

A huge white horse walks into a bar, leans his hooves on the counter, and asks for a beer. Serving him, the barman can't resist commenting, "You know, we've got a brand of whisky named after you."

"What, Eric Whisky?" says the horse. "Never heard of it."

•

What's green and hangs from trees?
   Giraffe snot.

•

A man suspects his wife of cheating on him, so he goes to the pet store to shop for a parrot. He sees quite an assortment for sale for $500 to $1000, but that's a bit more than he wants to spend, so he's delighted to come across one in the corner for sale for $29.95. "How come that one's so cheap?" he asks the clerk.

"To tell ya the truth, his dick's oversized and embarrasses the customers" is the explanation. The husband buys the bird anyway, and installs it on a perch right over the bed.

The next day the first thing he does after coming home from work is to rush upstairs. "Well, what happened today?" he demands of the bird.

"Well, the milkman came, and . . . your wife told him to come into the bedroom, and . . . they took off their clothes, and . . . got into bed."

"So what happened next," screams the irate husband.

"I don't know," says the parrot. "I got hard and fell off my perch."

•

"Mommy, Mommy, do we have to take the dog for a walk again?"

"Shut up and drive."

Why did the pervert cross the road?
Because his dick was stuck in the chicken.

•

One day this farmer was bragging to his neighbor that his dog was so smart he could count. Of course, the other farmer didn't believe him, so the first farmer ordered his dog to go down to the pond and count the geese. The dog took off, came back, and barked four times, and when the farmers walked down to the pond, sure enough there were four geese in sight.

Back at the farmhouse the neighbor confessed he was still sceptical, so the farmer sent the dog off again. This time the dog came back and barked six times, and sure enough there were six geese on the pond.

When the neighbor was still unsatisfied, the farmer agreed to test the dog one more time and off the dog ran. On his return he started humping his master's leg, then picked up a stick and started shaking it.

"I knew that fool dog couldn't count," said the neighbor triumphantly.

"Oh, yes, he can," said the farmer, "you just can't understand him. He just said there are more fucking geese than you can shake a stick at."

•

What did the doe say as she rushed out of the woods?
"I'll never do that for two bucks again!"

•

What do you do with a bird with no wings?
Take it for a spin.

What does a black parrot say?
  "Polly wanna white woman."

·

What do you call a person who can't walk through a pasture
without getting shit all over his shoes?
  An incowpoop.

MALE ANATOMY

What's the problem with oral sex?
The view.

•

One morning a milkman called on one of his regular customers and was surprised to see a white bedsheet with a hole in the middle hanging up in her living room. The housewife explained that she'd had a party the night before. They had played a game called "Who's Who" in which each of the men had put their equipment through the hole and the women tried to guess their identity.

"Gee, that sounds like fun," said the milkman. "Sure wish I'd been there."

"You should have been," said the housewife. "Your name came up three times."

•

A man with a two-inch prick walks into a whorehouse and drops his pants in front of one of the girls, who says, "Just who do you think you're going to please with that little thing?''

And the man says, ''Me.''

•

What did the flasher say to the woman in sub-zero weather?

''It's so cold—should I just describe myself?''

•

A man walks into his doctor's office and the receptionist gives him a form to fill out and asks him what his problem is. He says, ''I've got something wrong with my dick.''

''Please watch your language!'' scolds the receptionist. ''There are women and children in the waiting room.''

The would-be patient leaves the office, only to return a few minutes later and say to the receptionist, ''I've got a problem with my ear.''

''Now that's much better,'' says the receptionist. ''What's wrong with it?''

''I can't piss out of it.''

•

How do you say ''premature ejaculation'' in French?

''Ooh la la—so soon?''

•

The newlyweds were undressing in their honeymoon suite on the wedding night. The new husband, who was a big bruiser of a guy, tossed his pants over to his wife and said, ''Here, put these on.''

Puzzled, she pulled them on and said, ''These would fit two of me—I can't wear these pants.''

"That's right," said the husband, "and don't you forget it. I'm the one who wears the pants in this family."

With that the wife threw her pants over to his side of the bed and said, "Try these on."

Finding he could only get them up as far as his knees, her husband said, "Hell, I can't even get *into* your pants."

"That's right," she snapped, "and that's the way it's going to be until your goddamn attitude changes."

•

What makes a man think he's so great?
   —He has a bellybutton that won't work.
   —He has tits that won't give milk.
   —He has a cock that won't crow.
   —He has balls that won't roll.
   —He has an ass that won't carry a thing.

Hey, what are you smiling for? Your pussy won't catch mice.

•

Did you hear about the guy with five dicks?
   His pants fit like a glove.

•

Little Billy asked his father, "Dad, what's a penis?"

Without missing a beat, his father unzipped his fly, pulled it out, and said, "Son, *this* is a penis. And, I might add, it's a perfect penis."

"Thanks, Dad," said little Billy, and ran over to his best friend's house to tell him about this new revelation.

"Really?" said his friend in amazement. "Well, what did he show you?"

"This," said the little boy, unzipping his own pants and taking out his prick. "And you know what? If it were just a little bit shorter, it'd be just as perfect as my dad's."

•

Why did God make man first?

He didn't want a woman looking over his shoulder.

•

A married woman is entertaining her lover one rainy afternoon when her husband unexpectedly comes home early from work. "Quick, out on the roof," hisses the woman, pushing him out the bedroom window and closing it just as her husband's footsteps reach the top of the stairs.

Crouched on the roof in the rain, the boyfriend is naked except for a rubber and is wondering what the hell his next move should be. The first person in sight is a jogger and the boyfriend takes a deep breath, jumps off the roof, and falls into step alongside the jogger as nonchalantly as possible. After a block and a half the jogger can no longer contain his curiosity and asks, "Say, you always wear that thing when you run?"

"Naw," says the boyfriend coolly, "only when it rains."

•

A recent poll uncovered the fact that 90% of all men masturbate in the shower. The other 10% sing. Do you know what they sing?

—You say you don't know? I didn't think so . . .

•

A traveling salesman was looking for a place to spend the night, and a local farmer offered to take him in if he didn't mind sharing quarters with his daughter. The salesman said that would be fine.

A few months later the salesman received the following letter from the farmer:

> Are you the guy who did the pushin'?
> Left the grease spots on the cushion?
> Left the footprints on the dashboard upside down?
> Ever since you left my Nellie
> She's been swellin' round the belly

So you'd better come back to this here town.

The salesman replied by return mail:

> Yes I'm the guy who did the pushin'
> Left the grease spots on the cushion
> Left the footprints on the dashboard upside down.
> Ever since I left your Venus
> I've been itching round the penis,
> So I think we're pretty even all around.

•

What's long and red and hard and comes with balls?
  A sequoia baseball bat.

•

A little girl walked into the bathroom, saw her father in the shower, and ran to her mother screaming, "Mommy, Mommy! Daddy has a big ugly worm hanging out of his weewee!"

"That isn't a worm, sweetheart," said her mother reassuringly. "That's part of your daddy's body and a very important part. If your daddy didn't have one of those, you wouldn't be here. And come to think of it . . . neither would I."

•

Having been at sea for three months, the sailor was extremely horny when they reached port. Heading straight to the nearest whorehouse, he asked the price.

"Seventy-five bucks," replied the madam. It seemed a pretty steep price to the sailor, but he paid up and was shown to a room to await the girl. When the whore opened the door, she saw the sailor masturbating furiously on the bed. "Stop, stop," she cried. "What're you doing?"

"Hey, for seventy-five bucks you don't think I'm going to let you have the easy one, do you?"

What do you call a two-hundred-foot rubber?
   A condominium.

·

One day Little Herbie heard a noise from his parents' room
and opened the door to see them screwing. "What're you
doing, Dad?" he asked.

"Just playing gin rummy with your mother," was the
answer.

On the way back downstairs, Little Herbie heard a noise
coming from his grandparents' room, opened the door, and
asked what was going on. His granddad explained he was just
playing gin rummy with his grandmother.

Not too much later, dinner was served and everyone came to
the table but Little Herbie. Looking in his room, Herbie's
father found him lying on his bed, the sheets flapping up and
down. "I'm just playing gin rummy," explained the boy.

"But you've got no one to play with," said his dad sternly.

"That's okay, Dad; with a hand like this, you don't need a
partner."

·

A farmer needed help as he realized his manhood was failing
him, so he asked his doctor for a cure. The doctor gave him a
small container of pills and told him to take no more than one
a week. Back at the farm, the farmer thought he'd try the
medication out on his stud horse first. The horse swallowed
the pill, jumped out of his stall, kicked a side of the barn
down, and ran off down the road. "Those pills are too strong
for me," the farmer thought and he poured the rest into the
well.

Later, when the doctor asked the farmer how the pills were
working, the farmer said he had thrown them down the well.
"Heavens!" the doctor exclaimed. "You haven't drunk any
of the water, have you?"

"No," the farmer said, "we can't get the pump handle
down."

·

One day when the teacher walked to the chalkboard, she noticed someone had written the word PENIS in tiny letters. She turned around and scanned the class looking for a guilty face. Finding none, she quickly erased it and began class.

The next day she went into the room and noticed in larger letters, written about halfway across the board, the word PENIS. Again, she looked around in vain for the culprit, so she proceeded with the day's lesson.

Every morning for about a week, she went into the classroom and found the word PENIS written on the board, each day's letters larger than the previous one's. Finally, one day, she walked in expecting to find the word PENIS on the board and found instead the words: "The more you rub it, the bigger it gets."

•

Sam, the butcher, wants desperately to try to impress a beautiful lady customer, so one morning when she walks in he says, "Good morning, what can I do for you this lovely day?"

The woman replies sternly, "Give me some of that prime rib that's on special."

Sam hurriedly shuffles around behind the counter. "It's been a long time since you've been by the shop," he says, the eagerness mounting in his voice, "so today, I'll do something special for you; I won't put my thumb on the scale!"

To that, the pretty customer replies coldly, "Sam, dear, if your dick were as big as that thumb, I'd buy my meat here all the time."

•

A carpenter, an electrician, and a dentist had a mutual friend who was getting married, and in keeping with the custom, each was determined to play a practical joke on the newlyweds.

The electrician decided to wire up the marriage bed so that when the two bodies touched, they got a shock. The carpenter planned to saw partly through the bed frame so that it would collapse when the shocked newlyweds jumped apart. And as the wedding approached, the dentist was still scratching his head and trying to come up with something.

After the honeymoon the new husband confronted his three friends. "I didn't mind too much when we got zapped," he told them, "and we both got a good laugh when the bed fell down. But who the hell put Novocain in the Vaseline?"

•

A Scotsman stopped off for a few drinks at his local pub. On his way home he was having trouble navigating, so he decided to take a little rest by the roadside. As he was snoring gently, two girls came by and one said to the other, "You know, they say Scotsmen go naked under their kilts—shall we see if it's true?"

Her companion eagerly agreed, and when they lifted his kilt they found the story to be true indeed. In fact, what greeted their eyes was so pleasing that one of the girls took her blue hair ribbon and tied it around the man's dick as he slept.

Not too much later the Scotsman awoke, and when he stood up to take a pee he got quite a start at the sight of the blue ribbon. "Hoot mon!" he exclaimed. "I don't know what you've been up to, but I'm certainly glad to see you took first place."

•

Why is it only women get hemorrhoids?

Because when God created man, He created the perfect asshole.

One day Bobby's teacher tells the class they're going to play a thinking game, and asks for a volunteer. "Pick me, pick me," begs Bobby.

"Okay, Bobby," says the teacher. "Now I'm going to describe objects to you and you tell me what they are. Here we go: what's red, shiny, and you eat it?"

"A cherry," says Bobby.

"No, it's an apple, but it shows you're thinking," said the teacher gently. "Ready for the next one? What's yellow and you eat it?"

"A lemon," says Bobby.

"No," says the teacher, "it's a banana, but it shows you're thinking."

Before the teacher can continue, Bobby interrupts. "Okay, teacher, I've got one for you." He reaches into his pocket, looks down, pulls his hand out, and asks, "What's long, pink, and has a little red head on the end of it?"

"Ooh, Bobby!" squeals the teacher.

"No, it's a match—but it shows you're thinking."

•

One day this guy woke up to find that he had three bright red circles around the base of his penis. Panicked, he rushed to the doctor, thinking he'd contracted some new kind of herpes or V.D. The doctor was equally puzzled by the symptoms, gave the guy a course of antibiotics, and told him to come back in a week if the rings didn't clear up.

A week later the guy was back in the doctor's office but the second dose of medication had no effect either. On his third visit, the doctor told the guy to try various creams, soaps, and lotions. The next day the patient was back. "It worked, it worked!" he announced ecstatically.

"Oh, really? And what did you use to get rid of the rings?" asked the doctor.

"Lipstick remover."

Three friends were out enjoying a night on the town, and the suggestion that they visit the local whorehouse met with enthusiasm all around—especially when the madam told them there was a special offer that evening. For $100, $150, or $200, the customer would receive a sexual treat beyond his wildest dreams.

The first guy forks out $100, is shown to the first door on the right, and soon his friends hear cries of ecstasy coming from within. He emerges some time later, still sweaty and out of breath and grinning from ear to ear. "She's the most beautiful woman I've ever seen," he says happily, and goes on to explain that after extensive foreplay she had put two pineapple rings around his penis and eaten them.

The second guy can hardly wait to fork over his $150, is shown to a room, and soon wild cries of bliss can be heard. Eventually he returns with the same grin and the same story, except that he had gotten whipped cream along with the two pineapple rings.

The third guy needs little persuading to part with his $200 and is shown to an upstairs room. Soon cries of ecstasy can be heard, but his friends are puzzled when they're interrupted by a scream of agony. When he returns, they can't wait to hear what happened. Yes, he explained wearily, she was the most beautiful woman he'd ever seen, and after extensive foreplay she had covered his prick with two pineapple rings, whipped cream, chopped nuts, and topped it off with a maraschino cherry.

"So then what happened?" ask his friends eagerly.

"Well," he replied, "it looked so good I ate it myself."

•

What's green and used to fry pricks?
A Peter Pan.

•

There was this guy who desperately wanted to have sex with his girlfriend. However, he was too embarrassed because of his extremely small penis. So one night, he took her to a dark place where she couldn't see it and, after furiously making out with her, dropped his pants and put his penis in her hand.

"Sorry, I don't smoke," she whispered.

FEMALE ANATOMY

What do you call a four-foot woman in the Navy?
  A microwave.

•

As the newlywed couple was checking into the hotel for their honeymoon, another couple at the desk offered to show them around the town that night. Thanking them for the kind offer, the bridegroom explained that it was their wedding night and that they'd prefer to take a rain check.

When the second couple came down to breakfast the next morning they were astonished to catch sight of the groom in the hotel bar apparently drowning his sorrows. "Why, you should be the happiest man in the world today," they said, coming over to him.

"Yesterday I was," said the man mournfully, "but this morning, without realizing it, I put three ten-dollar bills on the pillow and got up to get dressed."

"Hey, cheer up, she probably didn't even notice."

"That's the problem," the groom went on. "Without even thinking, she gave me five dollars change."

Fred came home from work in time to catch his wife sliding naked down the banister. "What the hell are you doing?" he demanded.

"Just heating up dinner, darling," she cried.

•

Definition of vagina:
  The box a penis comes in.

•

Definition of rape:
  Piece without negotiations.

•

How do you start a fire without any matches?
  Hold a piece of toilet paper behind a fat girl wearing corduroys.

•

A pretty woman moved into town. She was so resistant to any advances by the local menfolk that they decided there must be something wrong with her sexual apparatus, maybe that she was a hermaphrodite. One guy finally talked her into going out to a movie with him, and was delighted when on the drive back she explained she urgently had to go to the bathroom. As she squatted in the bushes beside the car, he figured this was his chance to check out her anatomy, and snuck around the rear. Sure enough there was a long thing hanging down between her legs, and he reached out and grabbed it. "So!" he exclaimed weakly.

"You didn't tell me you were a Peeping Tom," she said tartly.

"And you didn't tell me you had to take a shit."

What's red, lives in a cave, and only comes out during sex?
  (Stick out your tongue.)

•

What's the difference between worry and panic?
  About twenty-eight days.

•

A certain virginal and shy college freshman was lucky to have a roommate who was considerably more experienced. When the bashful boy broke down and explained his predicament, his roommate was quick to offer to set him up with the campus floozie. "Just take her out to dinner and a show and then let nature take its course," he explained reassuringly. "This girl knows what the score is."

The roommate arranged the date as promised, and the freshman took the coed out for a delightful evening of dining and dancing. On the way home he parked his car in a dark lane, broke out in a cold sweat, and blurted out, "Gosh, I sure would love to have a little pussy."

"I would, too," she sighed. "Mine's the size of a milk pail."

•

During intercourse a husband had a heart attack and died. The next day the mortician informs the wife that the corpse still had a hard-on and he thought it would look odd in the coffin. "Fine," says the wife. "Cut if off and stick it up his ass." Making absolutely sure he'd heard correctly, the mortician obliges her.

During the funeral a number of the deceased's friends and relations are perturbed to see a tear in the corner of his eye, but the widow assures them there's no cause for concern. Just before the casket is closed, she leans over and quietly whispers in her dead husband's ear, "It *hurts*, doesn't it?"

•

A man called his wife from the hospital to tell her he'd cut his finger off at the assembly line. "Oh, honey," she cried, "the whole finger?"

"No," he said, "the one next to it."

•

An old lech walked into a bar and ordered a whisky. "What kind of whisky, sir?" asked the bartender politely.

"I take my whisky like I take my women," was the answer, "twelve years old."

•

The retired colonel walked into the Officers' Club and ordered a coffee. "How do you take your coffee, sir?" inquired the waiter.

"Hot, strong, and sweet," roared the colonel.

"Yes, sir, and will that be black or white?"

•

Definition of an orgasm:
  Gland finale.

•

In Dallas on business, Jerry picked up a lovely girl in the hotel bar and took her up to his room. After a few drinks, the girl sat on his lap. "Would you like to hug me?" she asked.

"Of course," panted Jerry, pulling her close.

"And would you like to kiss me?"

''You bet,'' said Jerry, planting a long kiss on her lips.

''Okay, honey,'' she continued, ''brace yourself, because here comes the fifty-dollar question.''

•

What's the difference between a woman in church and a woman in the bathtub?

A woman in church has hope in her soul.

•

What's the difference between an Italian woman and Bigfoot?

One is six feet tall, covered with matted hair, and smells terrible; the other has big feet.

•

A gigolo marries an ugly, not too bright woman who happens to have loads of money.

One day the man goes out to repair a hole in the roof of the stable. ''I'll need a ladder,'' he says to his wife.

''Get the ladder, get the ladder,'' she repeats dutifully as she trots off.

''I'll need a hammer and nails,'' he tells her a bit later.

''Get the hammer, get the nails, get the hammer . . .'' as she runs back to the tool shed.

The guy gets down to work and is hammering away when he hits himself squarely on the thumb. *''Fuck!''* he screams.

His wife bobs away, saying, ''Get the bag, get the bag!''

•

How can you tell if a woman isn't wearing pantyhose?

If, when she farts, she gets dandruff on her shoes.

A man and his wife were fooling around when she asked, "Honey, could you take your ring off? It's hurting me."

Her husband replies, "Ring, hell, that's my wristwatch."

•

This woman goes to the gynecologist for the first time and is rather embarrassed as she puts her feet in the stirrups. The doctor goes around for a look and says, "Why, that's the biggest pussy I've ever seen—the biggest pussy I've ever seen!"

"You didn't have to say it twice," snaps the woman.

"I didn't," says the doctor.

•

Why is rape so rare?

Because a woman can run faster with her dress up than a man with his pants down.

•

A Texan comes into a bar and it only takes him a few drinks to start boasting about the superior size of just about everything in Texas. "Did you know our women have tits forty feet across?" he asks proudly.

"Oh, really," says the man next to him politely.

"Well, they only miss it by this much," allows the Texan, holding his fingers about two inches apart. "And our women have cunts so big they can hold a dick twenty feet long."

"No kidding."

"Well, not quite, but they only miss it by about this much," says the Texan, indicating another two inches.

"Say, I bet you didn't know that the women in these parts have babies out their assholes," offers the local man.

"Is that so?" says the Texan, astonished.

"Well, not really, but they only miss it by about this much . . ."

What's the worst thing about having a cold when you've got your period?
  Having your tampon pop out when you sneeze.

•

Why do women have longer fingernails?
  Deeper penetration.

•

Know how to make a pussy talk?
  Put a tongue in it.

•

A nymphomaniac goes to the supermarket and gets all hot and bothered eyeing the carrots and cucumbers. By the time she gets to the checkout line she can't hold out much longer, so she asks one of the supermarket baggers to carry her groceries out to the car for her. They're halfway across the lot when the nympho slips her hand down his pants and whispers, "You know, I've got an itchy pussy."
  "Sorry, lady," says the bagger, "but I can't tell one of those Japanese cars from another."

•

Where do women airline pilots sit?
  In the cuntpit.

•

Why did the woman with the huge pussy douche with Crest?
  She heard it reduces cavities.

•

What do you call a female sex-change operation?
  An addadicktome.

What's the difference between eating pussy and eating sushi?
   The rice.

•

What's the difference between a woman and a volcano?
   Volcanos don't fake eruptions.

•

Two whores are walking down the street.
   One remarks, "I smell cock!"
   The other replies, "That's just my breath."

•

A wife arriving home from a shopping trip was horrified to find her husband in bed with a lovely young thing. Just as she was about to storm out of the house, her husband stopped her with these words: "Before you leave, I want you to hear how this all came about. While I was driving along the highway, I saw this young girl here, looking tired and bedraggled, so I brought her home and made her a meal from the roast beef you had forgotten in the refrigerator. She had only some worn-out sandals on her feet, so I gave her a pair of good shoes you had discarded because they had gone out of style. She was cold, so I gave her the sweater I bought you for your birthday that you never wore because the colors didn't suit you. Her slacks were worn out, so I gave her a pair of yours that were perfectly good but too small for you now. Then, as she was about to leave the house, she paused and asked, 'Is there anything else your wife doesn't use anymore?' "

•

What do you give a hooker on her birthday?
   A layer cake.

A newlywed couple had just left for their honeymoon. Almost there, Victoria asked Kenny if they'd stop so she could go to the bathroom. Since they were so close, Kenny told her to wait and Victoria agreed. About ten minutes later, she again asked him to stop, and again, he told her to wait. After about five more minutes, she was desperate and told him she couldn't wait one minute longer. Not wanting to stop, he told her to roll down the window and pee, which she did. Meanwhile, two hitchhikers, spotting the car, thumbed for a ride. Just as the car passed, Victoria peed out the window, hitting one of the hitchhikers in the face.

"Did you see the gob that guy spit in my face?" said the soaking wet hitchhiker to his companion.

"That's nothing," responded his friend. "You should have seen his lips!"

•

A woman went to the gynecologist and was told she was in perfect health and had the body of an eighteen-year-old. She was so excited she ran home to tell her husband.

"What about your fat ass?" he asked.

"He didn't say anything about you," she answered.

•

THE CREATION OF A PUSSY

Seven wise men with knowledge so fine,
    created a pussy to their design.
First was a butcher, smart with wit,
    using a knife, he gave it a slit.
Second was a carpenter, strong and bold,
    with a hammer and chisel, he gave it a hole.
Third was a tailor, tall and thin,
    by using red velvet, he lined it within.
Fourth was a hunter, short and stout,
    with a piece of fox fur, he lined it without.

Fifth was a fisherman, nasty as hell,
  threw in a fish and gave it a smell.
Sixth was a preacher whose name was McGee,
  touched it and blessed it and said it could pee.
Last came a sailor, dirty little runt,
  he sucked it and fucked it and called it a cunt.

•

Bumper sticker: Save the whale—harpoon a fat chick.

HOMOSEXUALS

Three white guys and two black guys are hanging out at the corner bar and get into an argument over whose dick is bigger. Finally they realize there's only one way to resolve the dispute, so they walk over to a table and lay them all out. Just then a fag walks in, takes one look, and squeals, "Ooh, a buffet."

•

What did one gay sperm say to the other?
  "How'm I supposed to find an egg in all this shit?"

•

What are cowboys who ride sidesaddle?
  Gay caballeros.

•

What's a fag's favorite expression?
  "Get ahold of yourself!"

What did the lesbian say as she guided her girlfriend's tongue toward her clitoris?

"This bud's for you."

•

Why was the fag disappointed in his long-awaited trip to London?

He found out Big Ben was a clock.

•

What's the definition of a bisexual?

Someone who likes girls as well as the next guy.

•

"In the center ring," cries the ringmaster, "we have Nero, the boldest and bravest animal trainer in the world. Watch, ladies and gentlemen, as he puts his head between the jaws of our man-eating lion!" The crowd roars as Nero pulls out his head unscathed.

"Now, folks, watch this!" shouts the announcer, as Nero unzips his pants and puts his prick between the giant teeth. "Don't do it!" shrieks the audience as the lion's jaws clamp shut. But without flinching, Nero pulls them open and removes his unharmed penis, and wild cheers fill the arena.

When the noise dies down the ringmaster steps forward and announces, "Ladies and gentlemen, a prize of five thousand, yes, five thousand dollars, to the man in our audience who'll try that trick." His jaw drops as a small, effeminate man steps right up to the ringside. "You're going to repeat that trick with our man-eating lion in front of all these people?" he asks incredulously.

"Certainly," says the fag, "but I must tell you something first. I don't think I can open my mouth as wide as the lion did."

•

What's this? [Stamp one foot up and down, and bow your head and blow.]

A fireman giving artificial resuscitation to a fag with AIDS.

•

Did you hear about Calvin Klein's jeans for fags?

They have knee pads in the front and a zipper in the back.

•

What do you get when you cross a black with a homosexual?

An AIDS victim with sickle-cell anemia.

•

One Sunday in church, a homosexual decided to make a ten-dollar contribution as the collection plate went by. Seeing his generosity, the preacher said, ''Brother, we'll let you pick out the next three hymns.''

The homosexual stood up and said, ''Oh, goody! I'll take him . . . and him . . . and him.''

•

''My dildo can do anything a man can do,'' boasted a dyke in a bar one night.

''Oh, yeah?'' replied a nearby drunk. ''Let's see your dildo get up and order a round of drinks.''

•

What's the difference between a hematologist and a urologist?

A hematologist pricks your finger . . .

•

What do you call a homosexual in a sleeping bag?

Fruit Roll-Up.

Why did they kick the fags out of Heaven?
  They were blowing all the prophets.

•

How can you tell the gay guy in biology class?
  While everyone else is dissecting frogs, he's opening flies.

•

Did you hear about the gay judges who tried each other?

•

How about the gay plastic surgeon who hung himself?

•

What do you call four fags in a custom van?
  The AIDS team.

•

What did the gay masochist say in the bar?
  "Any man in the house can whip me."

•

How can you spot sadists?
  They do nice things for masochists.

•

How can you spot masochists?
  They cry.

•

How can you spot those who are both?
  They do themselves a favor and then hate themselves for it.

How do you spot a black masochist?
He works for a living.

How do you spot a masochistic garbageman?
He doesn't hold his nose.

How do you spot a masochistic Polish garbageman?
He does.

•

Why didn't the masochistic little boy jack-off?
His mother caught his older brother at it and said, "If you hadn't gotten so big, I'd spank you."

•

What do you call a gay midget?
A low blow.

•

One night Fred came home from work and told his wife over dinner that he had just signed up with the company hockey team. Worried that he might hurt himself, his wife went out the next day to buy him a jockstrap.

The effeminate sales clerk was only too happy to help her. "They come in colors, you know," he told her. "We have Virginal White, Ravishing Red, and Promiscuous Purple."

"I guess white will do just fine," she said.

"They come in different sizes, too, you know," said the clerk.

"Gee, I'm really not sure what Fred's size is," confessed his wife. So the clerk extended his pinkie.

"No, it's bigger than that."

The clerk extended a second finger.

"No, it's bigger than that," said the wife.

A third finger.

"Still bigger," she said.

When the clerk stuck out his thumb, too, she said, "Yes, that's about right."

So the clerk put all five fingers in his mouth, pulled them out, and announced expertly, "That's a medium."

•

What do you call a gay who gets a vasectomy?
    A seedless fruit.

•

How can you tell if a termite is gay?
    He only eats male boxes.

•

What do you call a gay beautician and a gay pharmacist?
    Health and Beauty AIDS.

•

What do you call rubber sheets?
    Golden shower curtains.

•

What do you call a bouncer in a gay bar?
    A flamethrower.

•

What do you call a homosexual in jail?
    Canned fruit.

•

What's a gay bartender's favorite drink?
    Fruit cocktail.

What do you call a faggot in the navy?
  A Rear Admiral.

•

What does a deaf homosexual get?
  Hearing AIDS.

RELIGIOUS

A priest, a minister, and a rabbi are all enjoying a beer together when a fly lands right in the priest's glass. Fishing it out, the priest shakes off the fly and throws it in the air, saying, "Be on your way, little creature."

Five minutes later the fly is back, this time making a nosedive for the minister's beer. Fishing it out and shaking it dry, the minister tosses it in the air, saying, "Be free, little bug."

But the fly is a slow learner and ends up five minutes later in the rabbi's glass. Picking it up and shaking it violently, the rabbi screams, "Spit it out, spit it out!"

•

A young pastor married a girl who'd been around with lots of guys while he himself had little sexual experience. On their wedding night he stepped into the bathroom to put on his pajamas, and when he came out he was shocked to find his new wife lying nude on the bed. Alarmed, he blurted out, "I thought I would find you on your knees by the side of the bed"

"Nah," she said, "that position always gives me the hiccups."

•

What did Jesus say while hanging on the cross?
"This is a hell of a way to spend Easter vacation."

•

It's the eve of Pontius Pilate's birthday and his guards are sitting around trying to figure out something really special for the event. Finally they hit on a great idea: they'll nail all the Jews in the land up on crosses and use them to line the road to Pilate's house.

The next morning all the guards crowd around Pilate to wish him happy birthday and urge him to come outside. When he does, he's amazed and touched by the spectacle and begins to stroll down the road. At the very end he notices Jesus, King of the Jews. Unlike the rest, Jesus is still conscious and appears to be mumbling something, so since the King of the Jews might be saying something important, Pilate commands a ladder to be leaned up against the cross.

Climbing up and putting his ear to Jesus's lips, Pilate hears him mumbling, "Happy birthday to you, happy birthday to you . . ."

•

During Bible Study class Freddie was much more interested in his new hot rod car than in the lesson. His fidgeting didn't escape the Sister's notice, so she decided to give him a spot quiz. "Who was God's son, Freddie?" she asked.

The girl behind Freddie poked him hard with her pencil and he cried out, "Jesus!"

"Very good," said the Sister. "Now, who is the first member of the Holy Trinity?"

The girl poked Freddie even harder. "God Almighty!" he blurted.

"All right," said the Sister, deciding to throw him a trick question. "Now tell me what Eve said to Adam their first week together."

Once more the girl jabbed Freddie, and he screamed, "You prick me with that one more time and I'm going to shove it up your ass!"

•

An ambitious new sales rep for Budweiser beer traveled all the way to Rome and managed to finagle an audience with the Pope himself. As soon as the two were alone together, he leaned over and whispered, "Your Holiness, I have an offer I think might interest you. I'm in a position to give you a million dollars if you'll change the wording in the Lord's Prayer to 'our daily beer.' Now whaddaya say?"

"Absolutely not," said the shocked Pontiff.

"Hey, I understand; it's a big decision," sympathized the salesman. "How about five million dollars?"

"I couldn't think of it," sputtered the Pope.

"I know it's a tough one. Tell you what—I can go up to fifty million dollars," proposed the salesman.

Asking him to leave the room, the Pope called in the Cardinal and whispered, "When does our contract with Pillsbury expire?"

•

What do nuns wear on dates?

A Cross Your Heart bra and No Nonsense stockings.

•

It was late at night when the nudist got a little hungry and decided to get a snack at the corner deli. He walked in, bought a pack of gum and a candy bar, and was heading for the door when three nearsighted nuns came in. And he was so embarrassed that he just froze.

One of the nuns walked up to him, squinted, and said, "This must be a new vending machine." Putting a quarter in his mouth, she pulled his dick and he stuck out the hand holding the pack of gum. The second nun did the same, and got the candy bar.

"I do like that new vending machine," said the first nun as they left the store. "I got a pack of gum."

The second nun agreed. "I got my favorite candy bar."

"That's funny," said the third nun, "all I got was hand lotion."

•

A priest and a rabbi were out playing golf one day when the priest looked at his watch and said, "Pardon me, rabbi, but I must leave to go hear confession."

"What is this 'confession?' " asked the rabbi.

"It's when I listen to my parishioners tell me their sins and I absolve them while they say a penance," explained the priest.

"How interesting. Mind if I come along and watch?" asked the rabbi.

"Come on," said the priest, and they both crowded into the priest's side of the confessional.

The first penitent, a woman, came in and said, "Bless me, Father, for I have sinned. I have had sex with a man three times."

"That's all right, my child," comforted the priest. "Put five dollars in the poor box and say three Hail Marys and you will be absolved."

In came a second woman. "Forgive me, Father, for I have sinned," she said, "because I have had intercourse with a man three times."

"Don't worry about it," soothed the priest. "Put five dollars in the poor box, say three Hail Marys, and you will be absolved."

"Say, this looks easy," said the rabbi. "Mind if I give it a try?"

"Be my guest," said the priest as a third woman entered

the confessional. "As long as they think it's me, they'll be forgiven."

"Forgive me, Father, for I have sinned," said the third penitent. "I have had sex with a man two times."

"Listen," said the rabbi, "go out and do it one more time. We're having a special today—three for five bucks."

•

What does a rapist give a nun?
   Unleavened head.

•

This drunk is weaving down Florida's I-95 when his reckless driving happens to come to the attention of a minister. Trying to prevent a tragedy, the minister picks up speed and attempts to get ahead of the car to slow it down. But being a law-abiding citizen, the minister isn't used to speeds above 45 mph and proceeds to lose control of his car, winding up in a gully on the side of the road.

Realizing what's happened, the drunk turns around and drives back to the wreck. "Shay, buddy, you okay?" he asks, peering in the car window.

"I'm fine, for the Lord rides with me," retorts the minister indignantly.

"Oh, yeah?" says the drunk. "Well, you better let him ride with me, cause you're gonna kill him."

•

A sixteen-year-old girl went to make her confession at the neighborhood church. Blushing slightly, she answered the priest's query: "Well, Father, my boyfriend and I were at this party and he was kissing me, but I was innocent." After a pause, she went on, "Then we got into his car and he started taking my clothes off, but I was innocent, Father." Hearing only a sceptical snort from the other side of the confessional, she continued, "His car is a Volkswagen and I was completely undressed, so he spread my legs and put them in those two leather straps above the windows, but I was innocent, Father, I swear it."

The priest couldn't take it any more and burst out, "Enough of this shit. *I'm* the innocent here—I didn't even know what those straps were for!"

•

What's black and white and red all over?

A nun with stab wounds.

•

A six-year-old happened to be pulling his brand new wagon past the parish priest when one of the wheels came off. "Goddammit!" cursed the kid.

"Young man," scolded the priest severely, "don't you ever say that again. If something goes wrong for you, say, 'Help me, Lord' instead, do you understand?"

"Okay, Father," said the kid. But the very next day a second wheel fell off just as the priest was walking by. "Goddammit!" exploded the kid.

"What did I tell you?" boomed the priest. "What are you supposed to say?"

"Okay, okay," said the kid. Two days later the remaining two wheels fell off as the priest was lurking in the bushes, listening carefully. "Help me, Lord," said the little boy, and all four wheels jumped back on the wagon.

"Goddammit!" said the astonished priest.

•

What do you call a nun who's also a lesbian?

A nun with a bad habit.

•

One night little Johnny finished his prayers with "God bless Grandma," and the very next day his grandmother kicked the bucket. Johnny told his family about his prayer but no one seemed to give it too much thought. A week later he ended his prayers with "God bless Grandpa," and the next day his grandfather died. The family was running a little scared by now, and when Johnny finished his prayers one night with "God bless Daddy," his mother thought maybe she better warn her husband about it.

All that night Johnny's dad couldn't sleep for worrying, and the next day he came home from work early. "I had a terrible day worrying about all this," he confided to his wife.

"You think you had a bad day," she said. "The mailman came to the door and dropped dead."

•

One morning the town priest greeted one of his parishioners who was walking by holding a butterfly. "I'm going to get some butter," the man explained. The priest raised his eyebrows but didn't say anything, and not much later he saw the man walking home with a pound of butter under his arm.

The next day the same guy passed by holding a horsefly, "I'm off to get myself a horse," he said. The priest decided not to say anything, and sure enough pretty soon he saw the guy riding home on horseback.

The next day the same fellow passed by holding a pussywillow. "Don't say a word," said the priest. "I'm coming with you."

•

This fellow goes into the Catholic church. "Bless me, Father, for I have sinned," he says to the priest in the confessional. "I have committed adultery."

"I must know the name of the woman before I can grant you absolution," says the priest. "Was it Mrs. McCaffrey, the butcher's wife?"

"No, no—and please don't ask me to reveal her name."

"I must know. Was it Mrs. O'Shaughnessy, the laundress?"

"No, it was not."

"Then perhaps it was Mrs. O'Brien from the market?"

"Certainly not," says the man, and leaves the confessional.

"Did you get absolved?" asked the friend who'd been waiting for him outside the church.

"No," he said, "but I got some good leads."

•

A rabbi and a priest were seated together on a plane. After a while, they started talking and the priest said, "Rabbi, I hope you don't mind my asking, but I'm curious; have you ever eaten pork?"

"Actually, yes, once I got drunk and temptation overcame me. I had a ham sandwich and, I hate to admit it, I enjoyed it," replied the rabbi. "Now, let me ask you, have you ever been with a woman?"

"Well," responded the priest, "I once got drunk and went to a whorehouse and purchased the services of a prostitute. I, too, quite enjoyed the experience."

"It's a lot better than a ham sandwich, isn't it?"

CHILD ABUSE

A man was telling his neighbor that he had a surefire method for putting his baby to sleep. "I toss it up in the air over and over," he explained.

"How does that help?" asked the neighbor.

"We have low ceilings."

•

What's red and dances?

A baby on a burner.

•

What's bloody, spins, and screams?

A baby with its hand caught in a fan.

•

What glows and can't scream?

A wet baby with its fingers in an electrical outlet.

What's blue and knocks on the window?
   A baby in a fish tank.

•

What's red and white and screams?
   A baby having an epileptic fit on a bed of nails.

•

Heard about the new remedy for child molesters?
   Incesticides.

•

"How'd you blow that tire?" asked Moe.
   "Ran over a milk bottle," explained Joe.
   "Didn't you see it?"
   "Damn kid had it hidden under his coat."

•

How do you play with a dead baby?
   Cut off its arms and legs and use it as a football.

•

What's black and blue and goes tha-dump, tha-dump?
   A baby in a dryer.

•

What's black and blue and goes swish, tha-dump, tha-dump?
   A baby going down an incinerator.

•

What did the doctors do when they took Baby Fae off the critical list?
   Put her on the Endangered Species list.

•

"Knock, knock"
  "Who's there?"
  "Baby Fae."
  "Baby Fae who?"
  "Baby Fae hoo, hoo, hoo . . ."

•

What did they do once they got Baby Fae off the respirator?
  Tried to get her down off the chandelier.

•

What did Baby Fae die of?
  Baboonic Plague.

OLD AGE

Whitney woke up in the middle of the night and cried until his mother came in to see what was the matter. "I have to make pee pee," wailed the little boy.

"All right," said his mother. "I'll take you to the bathroom."

"No," insisted Whitney, "I want Grandma."

"Don't be silly, I can do the same thing as Grandma," said his mother firmly."

"Uh-uh. Her hands shake."

•

At his annual checkup Bernie was given an excellent bill of health. "It must run in your family," commented the doctor. "How old was your dad when he died?"

"What makes you think he's dead?" asked Bernie. "He's ninety and going strong."

"Aha! And how long did your grandfather live?"

"What makes you think he's dead, doc? He's a hundred

and ten years old and getting married to a twenty-two-year-old in two weeks,'' retorted Bernie.

"At his age!'' exclaimed the doc. "Why's he want to get married to a twenty-two-year-old?''

"Doc,'' said Bernie, "what makes you think he *wants* to?''

•

Grandpaw was sitting on the front porch talking to his teenage grandson about growing old. "Why, Teddy,'' he wheezed, "I remember goin' courting in the old buggy. On the way home I'd have to put my dong under a spoke in the buggy wheel to keep from peeing in my face, imagine that.''

"Yeah? Go on, Grandpaw,'' urged Teddy.

"Well, at seventy-five, things are a bit different. Now I have to rest it on one of the spokes to keep from peeing on my feet.''

•

Did you hear about the fifty-year-old hooker?

She sat down on a barstool and fell all the way to the floor.

•

Wondering what to give the older man who has everything?

A portable freezer to make it hard in an emergency.

•

Two seventy-year-old virgins finally decided to tie the knot and to honeymoon in Miami. Once they reached the hotel suite the old woman asked, "Well, dear, how do we do it?''

"I'm not sure, my love, but I have an idea,'' answered the old gent. He proposed that she stand by the window and he by the door, and that they run toward each other and meet in the middle.

"That sounds wonderful, dear. I'm so proud of you,'' quavered his bride, and off they go.

A little while later one of the hotel busboys said to another, "Did you know there's an old man who fell out the window lying naked as a jaybird in the middle of the sidewalk?"

"Yup," answered the other busboy. "We're still trying to get the old lady off the doorknob."

•

What's the worst song to request at a Golden Agers' dance?
  "Taps."

•

This old couple is walking through the park one day when a bird flying overhead lets one drop right on the woman's head. "Quick, dear," she quavers, turning to her husband, "get me some toilet paper."

"Eh?" he says, looking at her. "What's the use—the bird's at least a half mile away by now."

•

An eager-beaver young real estate agent was doing his best to sell this old coot a condominium in Palm Beach. Having outlined its many attractions in detail, he confidently concluded his pitch: "And, Mr. Rosenblatt, this is an investment in the future."

"Sonny," croaked Mr. Rosenblatt, "at my age I don't even buy green bananas."

•

The girls in the whorehouse were frankly sceptical when a ninety-year-old man came in and put his money down on the front desk, but finally a good-hearted hooker took him up to her room. Imagine her suprise when he proceeded to make love to her with more energy and skill than any man she had ever known. "I've never come so many times," she gasped. "How about once more, on the house?"

"All right," conceded the old geezer, "but I have to take a

five-minute nap and you must keep your hands on my penis, just so, while I'm asleep." She agreed eagerly, and as soon as he woke up he gave her an even better lesson in lovemaking.

"Oh, God," gasped the hooker ecstatically, "I can't get enough of you. Please, just once more—I'll pay *you*."

The old man agreed, subject to the same conditions, and just before he nodded out, the hooker said, "Excuse me, but would you mind explaining about the nap and why I have to keep my hands on your privates?"

"I'm ninety years old," retorts the man, "so is it so surprising I need a little rest? As for the other, it's because the last time while I was napping, they took my wallet."

•

The old farmer and his wife were sitting on their porch after celebrating their fiftieth wedding anniversary. At long last the wife broke the peaceful silence with a question. "Have you ever been unfaithful to me?"

"Once, dear, just once," quavered her husband. "And you?"

"Just a minute," she said and disappeared into the house, returning with a shoebox containing six kernels of corn and twenty thousand dollars in cash.

Her husband looked at her and said, "What the hell does this mean?"

"Every time I'm unfaithful to you, I put a kernel of corn in the box," she explained.

"Well, what's the money for?"

His wife said, "Every time I get a bushel, I sell it."

MISCELLANEOUS

What do you get when you cross Continental and Aer Lingus?
  Connilingus.

·

What would you get if General Mills merged with Alitalia?
  Genitalia.

·

The wife was at home when the call came from the local brewery. "I'm afraid I have some tragic news, ma'am," said the brewery representative. "There's been a terrible accident: your husband has drowned in a vat of beer."

"Oh, my God," gasped the new widow. "Did he . . . did he suffer much?"

"I don't think so, ma'am—he got out to pee four times before he went under."

·

What do you call a woman who makes beds in no-tell motels?
  Minute Maid.

•

What's the definition of a metallurgist?
  A man who can tell if a platinum blonde is a virgin metal or a common ore.

•

What do they give a cannibal who is late for dinner?
  The cold shoulder.

•

A settler in the Midwest felt he had to protect his family from wild animals and unfriendly Indians—but he also needed to chop wood for the fire. So he bought a large bell and set it up outside, instructing his wife to ring it in case of an emergency.

The next day he was busy chopping wood when he heard the bell ring in the distance. Terrified, he grabbed his rifle and ran home, only to find his wife standing in the clearing holding a tray. "I baked you some cookies, honey," she said.

Patiently he explained that the bell was only for a real emergency, and went back to chopping wood. Just a few days later the bell rang again and he rushed back, only to be shown a wounded bird his son had brought home. This, he made clear a little less patiently, was not his idea of a dangerous emergency.

A week later he rushed home at the clang of the bell. Reaching the clearing, he found that the house had been felled by a tornado, his wife had been murdered and scalped by Indians, and wildcats were gnawing the bloody remains of his children.

"Now, this is more like it!" said the settler.

•

Hear about the new combination aphrodisiac and laxative?
   It's called "Easy come, Easy go."

•

Deciding it was time for a history review, the teacher asked the class, "Who can tell me what historical figure said, 'I have not yet begun to fight'?"
   The little Japanese girl in the front row raised her hand and answered, "John Paul Jones."
   "Very good, Miyako. Now, who can tell me who said, 'I regret that I have but one life to give for my country?' "
   Again the little Japanese girl was the only one to raise her hand, and piped up, "That's Nathan Hale."
   The teacher said to the class, "What's going on? So far Miyako's the only one to answer any of my questions."
   Suddenly a voice was heard from the back of the room. "Aw, fuck the Japanese!"
   "Who said that?" asked the teacher sharply.
   Miyako's hand shot up. "Lee Iacocca!" she said brightly.

•

What is another name for Jell-O?
   Kool-Aid with a hard-on.

•

What do coffins and condoms have in common?
   They both have stiffs in them, but one's coming and one's going.

•

What did the mad rapist who worked at AT&T say?
   "Reach out and touch someone."

Did you hear about the sailor who got sucked under the dock by a wave?

•

Hear about the man who went to bed with his sister-in-law?
  He had it in for his brother.

•

What do you call 100 singing idiots drinking diet soda and eating fruit?
  The Moron Tab and Apple Choir.

•

What would you rather be, a light bulb or a bowling ball?
  Depends on whether you'd rather be screwed or fingered.

•

An angry mother took her son to the doctor and asked, "Is a nine-year-old boy able to perform an appendectomy?"
  "Of course not," the doctor said impatiently.
  The mother turned to her son and said, "What did I tell you? Now put it back."

•

Two strangers met on a golf course and the conversation came around to their occupations. The first man said he was in real estate; in fact, he owned a condominium complex that was barely visible in the distance. The second man said he was a professional assassin, but his new acquaintance was sceptical until the man took some pipes out of his golf bag and assembled them into a rifle.
  "I'll be damned," said the first guy.
  "The best part of this rifle is the high-power scope," confided the assassin, handing him the gun.
  "You're right," said the first man. "I can see inside my

apartment with it. There's my wife . . . and she's in there with another man!'' Furious, he turned to the assassin and asked how much he charged for his services, to which the reply was, ''A thousand dollars a bullet.''

The man said, ''I want to buy two bullets. I want you to kill my wife with the first one and blow the guy's balls off with the second.''

Agreeing to the offer, the assassin looked through his scope and took aim. Then he lifted his head and said, ''If you'll hang on a minute, I can save you a thousand dollars.''

•

Two cannibals came upon a dead body. In order to make sure that both would get equal portions, the big cannibal said to the little cannibal, ''You start at the head and I'll start at the feet.''

Not much later the little cannibal looked up and exclaimed, ''Man, I'm having a ball.''

The big cannibal replied, ''Slow down, you're going too fast.''

•

What's the definition of ''hijacking''?

A masturbating astronaut.

•

It's late at night when a spaceship lands in the middle of nowhere in central Iowa. The Martians—who look kind of like your average gas pump, not exactly but pretty close— descend from the ship and begin looking for signs of intelligent life. Coming across a road they follow it until they come across a one-pump gas station, which looks somewhat like a Martian—not exactly, but pretty close.

The captain is overjoyed—this must be what they are seeking! Deciding to make contact, he intones to the pumps, ''Greetings. We come from planet Xjbzoldt in search of intelligent beings. Will you take us to your leader?'' When there's no response, he repeats his query as loudly as possible. Still no answer, so he turns to his voice translator. Finally, enraged by the lack of a reply, he whips out his laser gun and points it at the pump. "Why, you insolent son of a whore—take us to your leader or I'll blast you!" His lieutenant tries to stop him, but it's too late. The captain fires, and an immense explosion hurls the Martians a hundred feet in the air.

Three hours later they're coming to, the lieutenant helping the captain to his feet. In a shaky voice the captain asks, "Wha . . . what happened?

The lieutenant replies, "Look, Captain, if I told you once, I told you a hundred times: you just don't go messing with a guy who can wrap his prick twice around his waist and stick it in his ear."

•

What's white and goes up?
A retarded snowflake.

•

During summer vacation a pharmacist hired a schoolboy to wait on customers, deliver prescriptions, and run errands, but he told the boy never to dispense any medicine or give any medical advice. The boy worked out well and the pharmacist took to leaving him alone in the store during mealtimes.

One evening the pharmacist returned after a dinner break and asked the boy if there had been any customers. "Only one," said the boy, "a fellow who was sneezing three or four times a minute. So I had him drink a pint of castor oil."

"Oh, my God," said the druggist. "Where is he?"

"That's him standing over in the back of the store—now he's afraid to sneeze."

Why does the crack in your ass go up and down instead of across?

So that when you're sliding downhill, you don't mumble.

•

One day Count Dracula decided to take his summer vacation in Italy. He rented a suitable castle and every night he would capture a lovely Italian maiden, suck the blood from her body, and throw her off the ramparts into the moat. This went on for two weeks, until he noticed there was no longer any splash, so the next night he watched carefully as his victim fell toward the dark water.

Up reared a giant alligator which caught the body in mid-air. Leaning over, the Count was able to hear it singing, "Drained wops keep falling on my head . . ."

•

A cop on the beat came across a man with his finger stuck up another man's ass. "Hey, what's going on here?" asked the cop gruffly.

"This guy had too much to drink and I'm trying to make him throw up," was the explanation.

"Putting your finger in his asshole isn't going to do the trick," said the cop.

"No, but when I take it out and put it in his mouth it will!"

•

An attractive saleswoman was driving her car through Montana when she ran out of gas. Getting out of her car, she saw nothing in the barren countryside except a single rundown shack and, on closer inspection, two dim-looking country boys sitting on the front porch.

"Hey there, where's the nearest gas station?" asked the woman.

"Oh, 'bout twenty-five miles west as the crow flies," was the answer.

It was getting dark so the woman decided to take her chances and ask for a room for the night. "Fine with us . . . 'cept we only got one bed," said the second man with an evil leer.

"Okay," said the woman reluctantly, but when they were getting ready for bed, she added, "I can't help it if you two take advantage of me, but please wear these condoms." Looking as though they'd never seen rubbers before, the country boys put them on.

The next morning they gave the woman a gallon of gas and she went on her way. Three months later the guys were sitting on their porch and one says to the other, "Hey, Luke?"

"Yeah?"

"Do you really care if that lady gets pregnant?"

"Naw, not really."

"Then you think we can take these things off now?"

•

Graffiti: "Candy is dandy, but sex won't rot your teeth"

"Yeah, but M & M's won't give you herpes"

•

Three traveling salesmen ran out of gas not far from a hospitable farmer's house. He and his eighteen beautiful daughters invited them in out of the rain and said they could spend the night, although the farmer apologized for the fact that there was only one spare bedroom and two salesmen would have to sleep in the barn. The three salesmen gratefully accepted his offer, for there were no towing services available at that time of night.

The next morning the salesmen went on their way and in the car they began to compare notes about the evening's experience. "All I thought about was straw," said the first guy, "because I had to sleep with the horses."

"You think that's bad," piped up the second guy. "All I dreamed about was mud, because I was down there with the pigs. How 'bout you, Phil?"

"I'll tell ya," said Phil blearily, "all I could think about was golf."

"Why golf?" asked the driver.

"Hey, if you shot eighteen holes in one night, that's all you'd be able to think about either."

•

A prosperous stockbroker and his wife had everything money could buy, until the broker gambled on a few bad tips and lost everything. He came home with a heavy heart that night and said to his wife, "You better learn to cook, Myrna, so we can fire the cook."

His wife thought it over for a few moments and said, "Okay, but you better learn to screw, George, so we can fire the chauffeur."

•

The newlyweds stopped at a farmhouse and agreed to rent a room for the night. By noon the next day they were still not up and about, so the farmer yelled up that it was last call for breakfast.

"Don't worry about us," called the groom, "we're living on the fruits of love."

"Okay," screamed the farmer, "but quit throwing the damned skins out the window—they're choking the ducks."

•

How is making love in a canoe like a light beer?

They're both fucking close to water.

•

Once there were three city boys who decided to go camping for the week. They rented a cabin way up in the mountains and when they got there, one boy said, "Who's gonna cook?"

There were no volunteers so they drew straws, and the loser said, "Okay, I'll cook. But if anyone complains, they're taking over the cooking.'' Everyone agreed, and no one said a word when dinner that night was pretty terrible.

The next night the cook broiled the coffee, torched the steak, and puked in the milk, but still no one complained. He was pissed. The next day he came across a big pile of moose shit in the woods, came back to the cabin early, and made it into a delicious-looking pie. When his friends returned for dinner the pie was sitting in the middle of the table, and even though it smelled funny it looked great.

The greediest camper inhaled his dinner and cut himself a gigantic slice of the pie. Taking a giant bite, he opened his eyes about six inches wide and gasped, ''*Moose shit* . . . but good, but good!''

•

What's the difference between a baby and a choir director?

A baby sucks his fingers . . .

•

Finally admitting he was grossly overweight, this man decided it was time to take advantage of a special introductory offer from a new weight-loss clinic in town. After handing over his payment, he was shown into an empty room where he was soon joined by a gorgeous blonde. ''Hi,'' she said. ''If you catch me, I'm yours.''

It took a while, but after a prolonged chase he succeeded—and was delighted to find he'd lost ten pounds in the process. After that he gave up all ideas of dieting and managed to drop ten more pounds with a brunette and eight with a redhead. But he was still fifty pounds overweight, so he decided to sign up for the clinic's more drastic program. He was waiting eagerly in an empty room when the door opened and in came a three-hundred-pound gay leper who grinned and said, ''If I catch you, you're mine!''

•

What's 71?
  Sixty-nine with two fingers up your ass.
What's 72?
  Sixty-nine with three people watching.
So what's 69 and 69?
  Dinner for four.

•

This guy called up his lawyer to tell him he was suing for divorce and the lawyer inquired as to his grounds for the suit.
  "Can you believe my wife says I'm a lousy lover?" sputtered the husband.
  "*That's* why you're suing?" asked the lawyer.
  "Of course not. I'm suing because she knows the difference."

•

One night Judge O'Brien tottered into his house very late and very drunk indeed, so bombed that he had managed to throw up all over himself. In the morning he sheepishly told his wife that a drunk sitting next to him on the train home had managed to vomit all over him.
  The judge managed to make it in to the courthouse, where it occurred to him that his story might not be truly convincing to his wife. Inspired, he called home and said, "Honey, you won't believe this but I just had the drunk who threw up on me last night show up in court, and I gave him thirty days."
  "Give him sixty days," said the judge's wife. "He shat in your pants, too."

•

What the difference between a beer and a booger?
  You put a beer on the table and a booger under it.

•

A middle-aged man confided to his doctor that he was tired of his wife and wished there were some way of doing her in so that he could have some good years left to himself. "Screw her every day for a year," counseled the doctor. "She'll never make it."

As chance would have it, it was about a year later when the doctor happened to drop by his patient's house. On the porch sat the husband looking frail and thin; tan and robust, his wife could be seen out back splitting wood."

"Say, Sam, you're looking good," said the doctor uneasily, "and Laura certainly's the picture of health."

"Little does she know," hissed Sam with a wicked little smile, "she dies tomorrow."

•

Help bring some love into the world:
    Fuck someone today!

•

It's after dinner when this guy realizes he's out of cigarettes. He decides to pop down to the corner bar for a pack, telling his wife he'll be right back. The bartender offers him a draft on the house and he decides he has time for just one. He's nursing it along when a gorgeous blonde comes in the door, but he looks the other way because he knows he has no time to fool around. So can he help it if she comes and sits right next to him and says how thirsty she is?

One thing leads to another and eventually the girl says how much she likes him and invites him back to her apartment to get better acquainted. How can he refuse? They go back to her place and go at it like crazy, and the next thing he knows it's four o'clock in the morning. Jumping out of bed, the guy shakes the girl awake and asks if she has any baby powder.

"Yeah, in the bathroom cabinet," she says groggily.

He dusts his hands liberally with the powder, drives home at 90 mph, and pulls into the driveway to find his wife waiting up for him with a rolling pin in her hand. "So where've you been?" she screeches.

"Well, you see, honey," he stammers, "I only went out for cigarettes, but Jake offered me a beer and then this beautiful bombshell walked in and we got to talking and drinking and we've been back at her apartment fucking like bunnies . . ."

"Wait a minute," snaps his wife. "Let me see your hands." Turning on him furiously, she says, "Don't you *ever* try lying to me again, you rotten little skunk—you've been bowling again!"

•

Scott had had a crush on Liza for months, so he was filled with hope when she invited him home for dinner with her family. In fact he was so optimistic that he stopped off at the drugstore beforehand to pick up some condoms.

At dinner Scott was asked to say grace, and to Liza's surprise he prayed for a good ten minutes. "I didn't know you were religious," she whispered to him over the buttered peas.

"And I didn't know your father was a pharmacist," he hissed back.

•

A cowboy walks into a Dairy Queen with two .45's slung around him in a holster and orders a sundae from the waitress. She asks if he'd like whipped cream and he says yes. "How about hot fudge?" she asks.

"Yes, thanks."

"A cherry?"

"Yup."

"And nuts?"

"Yes."

The waitress goes off and starts making up the sundae, but she pops back with another question for the cowboy. "Would you like your nuts crushed?" she asks brightly.

"Fuck no," says the cowboy, drawing both his guns. "You want your tits blown off?"

•

What do you call a governess who farts?
  A hootenanny.

•

The town drunk wanders into a saloon and motions for the bartender to come over to him. The bartender finally does, and the drunk whispers loudly, "What you need is some entertainment in this dive. Tell ya what—you set me up with six whiskies and I'll get up on that stage and fart Dixie. The crowd'll go wild."

Being a good-natured type, the bartender agrees to the deal. The drunk downs the six whiskies with no trouble, and the bartender reminds him gently that it's time for "Dixie." "No problem," says the drunk, getting up from his stool and staggering onto the stage. There's a roar of approval from the crowd as he turns his back and pulls down his pants, but it turns into howls of dismay as the drunk proceeds to bend over and shit all over the floor. "What the hell do you think you're doing?" shouts the bartender.

The drunk retorts, "Hey, even Bing Crosby clears his throat before he sings."

•

A man goes to the U.S. Patent Office and asks to patent the apple he's carrying. "You can't do that," says the Patent Office offical. "Mother Nature invented the apple."

"Not this apple; it's special," says the man. "Take a bite."

The officer takes a bite and says, "So? It tastes like any old apple."

"Turn it around, turn it around."

"Wow—it tastes like a pear!"

"Turn it again."

"This is incredible," says the official, "it tastes like a peach." And he gives the guy a patent on his three-flavored apple.

As the man's walking through the lobby on his way out, he

comes across a man with a bagful of cookies. "What've you got there?" he asks cheerfully.

"Special cookies," explains the second guy. "Take a bite and it tastes like pussy."

"I don't believe it—let me try one." He takes a big bite, only to make a face and sputter, "Goddamn, this tastes like *shit*."

"Turn it around, turn it around!"

•

There's a new solution to the welfare problem:
   AIDS for families with dependent children.

TOO TASTELESS
TO BE INCLUDED

What has no arms and no legs and costs us about $1000 a day?
   Baby Doe.

•

What's ruder than sending an anniversary card to Yoko Ono?
   Sending a Father's Day card to Charles Lindbergh.

•

What's worse than your dentist telling you you have herpes?
   Your mother telling you.

•

In a sleazy little back alley in a sleazy little town is a sleazy little restaurant with a sign that says SPECIALTY FOODS COOKED TO ORDER. One evening the maitre d' walks into the kitchen looking like he's seen a ghost. "Boss, you're not going to believe this," he says. "Somebody just sat down at table 3 and told me to bring him a bucket of warm shit."

"This isn't April Fool's Day," retorts the chef angrily. "I'm too tired for this."

"I'm not kidding. He wants a bucket of warm shit."

The cooks thinks it over for a minute or two, then says, "You name it, we cook it." Going to the utility closet he pulls out a scrub bucket and steps into the bathroom with it. Coming out, he orders each of the employees to make his or her contribution. Everyone obeys, the bucket is taken out and returned empty, and from time to time over the next few months the strange customer returns with the same order.

"It's him again," says the chef one night. He fills the bucket with help from customers and delivery men, and the maitre d' carries it out. Suddenly there's a wild commotion from the dining room, followed by the sound of a door slamming. The maitre d' returns, the bucket on his head, warm drops of shit dribbling down his shirtfront.

"He says he's never coming back, boss. There was a hair in it."

•

Did you hear about the Polish guy who ate pussy?
   He spit out the kittens after he was done.

•

Little Johnny came tearing into the kitchen, his finger all gooey and bloody, yelling with excitement, "Mommy, Mommy, I found the baby's soft spot."

•

How do you recondition an aging hooker?
   Shove a ten-pound ham up her and pull out the bone.

What's grosser than gross?

When your boyfriend wakes up with a lump in his throat and a string attached.

•

"Mommy, mommy, I don't like tomato soup."

"Shut up and eat—we only have it once a month."

•

What's red and screams?

A dead baby rolling in salt.

•

What's grosser than a thousand dead babies in a pile?

One eating its way out.

What's even grosser?

When it goes back for seconds.

•

A man goes into a whorehouse and makes an offer to the madam. "I don't have any money," he says, "but if I can guess how many men any of your girls have slept with so far today, I get to have her for an hour. How about it?"

Intrigued, the madam agrees to the proposal and calls her best girl, Pam. She takes the man up to her room and in two minutes he's back down at the front desk and announces, "Fourteen." Barely waiting until the madam has checked the register and confirmed the total, he skips upstairs and proceeds to have a grand old time with Pam.

In exactly an hour he comes back down and is heading out the door when the madam calls him over. "Just tell me," she asks, "how did you do it?"

"Easy," said the satisfied customer. "I drank her douche depository and counted the lumps."

How do you know when you've had a great blowjob?

You have to pull the sheets out of the crack in your ass.

•

A young pitcher was taking a few warm-up tosses from the mound when he noticed a beautiful brunette in the stands right in front of him with her legs spread wide. The pitcher could see a dark patch between her legs and began to wonder if the patch was her pussy or her panties. The game started, and by the second inning the pitcher was dying to know. Calling his catcher up to the mound, he said, "Say, man, there's this chick right behind you that has her legs open like crazy. Go up there and let me know if it's pussy or underwear."

The catcher went up eagerly into the stands, but when he came back he was puking his guts out and was taken off to the showers. Now the pitcher was really curious. At the bottom of the fifth he couldn't stand it any longer. Calling the shortstop over for a conference, he explained about the girl. "I'm going nuts, Bobby, I've gotta know whether it's pussy or panties. Will you check it out for me?"

The shortstop was more than willing. He took a quick time-out to run up into the stands, only to stagger back down white as a sheet, retching violently.

By the ninth inning the pitcher's curiosity was still unsatisfied, and he hit on a really reliable person, his manager. "Stan, I've had this problem the whole game," he said, explaining the situation. "Is it black panties or pussy?"

"Be right back," said his manager confidently. But he too was puking and pale as he stumbled back down to the field. He was heading for the showers when the pitcher simply couldn't stand it any more. Abandoning the mound, he ran over screaming desperately, "What was it? What was it? Pussy or underwear?"

The manager looked at him weakly. "Flies," he said.

•

A man went into a restaurant for lunch and ordered soup, mashed potatoes, milk, and coffee. When the waitress brought him the coffee she had her thumb in it, but the customer was too polite to say anything. Then she brought over his milk with her thumb stuck in the glass, and the same with his soup. Finally she served his meal, her thumb buried in his mashed potatoes, and he couldn't keep quiet any longer. "I hate to embarrass you," he said politely, "but when you served my coffee you had your thumb in it, and the same with my milk and soup and mashed potatoes."

"I know," said the waitress. "I have an infected thumb and the doctor said I should soak it as much as possible."

"That's revolting," said the customer, thoroughly grossed out. "Why don't you just stick it up your ass?"

"Oh, I do when I'm in the kitchen," she said.

Would you like to see your favorite tasteless jokes in print? If so, send them to:

Blanche Knott
c/o Pinnacle Books
1430 Broadway
New York, N.Y. 10018

PLUS

Having problems that may be too tasteless or too bizarre for your average advice columnist? Write c/o DEAR BLANCHE at the above address, and keep an eye out for DEAR BLANCHE: ADVICE FOR THE EIGHTIES, in your bookstore next year.

Remember, we're sorry but no compensation or credit can be given.

LAUGH ALONG WITH
Larry Wilde

"America's bestselling humorist."
— The New York Times

V
by A.C. Crispin
☐ 42237-7/$2.95 ☐ 43231-3/$3.50 (in Canada)

V: EAST COAST CRISIS
by Howard Weinstein and A.C. Crispin
☐ 42259-8/$2.95 ☐ 43251-8/$3.50 (in Canada)

V: THE PURSUIT OF DIANA
by Allen Wold
☐ 42401-9/$2.95 ☐ 43397-2/$3.50 (in Canada)

V: THE CHICAGO CONVERSION
by Geo. W. Proctor
☐ 42429-9/$2.95 ☐ 43417-0/$3.50 (in Canada)

V: THE FLORIDA PROJECT
by Tim Sullivan
☐ 42430-2/$2.95 ☐ 43418-9/$3.50 (in Canada)

V: PRISONERS AND PAWNS
by Howard Weinstein
☐ 42439-6/$2.95 ☐ 43420-0/$3.50 (in Canada)

V: THE ALIEN SWORDMASTER
by Somtow Sucharitkul
☐ 42441-8/$2.95 ☐ 43421-9/$3.50 (in Canada)

V: THE CRIVIT EXPERIMENT
by Alan Wold
☐ 42466-3/$2.95 ☐ 43441-3/$3.50 (in Canada)

V: THE NEW ENGLAND RESISTANCE
by Tim Sullivan
☐ 42467-1/$2.95 ☐ 43442-1/$3.50 (in Canada)

V: DEATH TIDE
by A.C. Crispin and D. Marshall
☐ 42469-8/$2.95 ☐ 43443-X/$3.50 (in Canada)

V: THE TEXAS RUN
by Geo W. Proctor
☐ 42470-1/$2.95 ☐ 43444-8/$3.50 (in Canada)